TWENTIETH
CENTURY
WORLD
HISTORY

THE MIDDLE EAST
IN THE TWENTIETH CENTURY

RICHARD I. LAWLESS

*Assistant Director, Centre for Middle Eastern
and Islamic Studies, University of Durham*

(with Heather Bleaney, Anne Findlay and David Imrie)

BATSFORD ACADEMIC AND EDUCATIONAL *London*

CONTENTS

ACKNOWLEDGMENT

The Author and Publishers thank the following for their kind permission to reproduce copyright illustrations: Associated Press for figs 18, 20, 40, 41, 48, 60; BBC Hulton Picture Library for figs 6, 7, 8, 9, 24, 36; Camerapix for fig 64; Camera Press Ltd for figs 12, 16, 38, 53, 56, 59, 71; Les Gibbard for fig 61; Imperial War Museum for fig 23; MEED Library for fig 54; The Middle East Magazine for fig 49; Middle East International for fig 42; Christine Osborne for fig 62; Popperfoto for figs 10, 11, 19, 25, 26, 27, 30, 31, 32, 33, 34, 35, 39, 44, 45, 46, 47, 52, 57, 67, 68; Rex Features Ltd for fig 66; UNWRA (Sue Herrick Crammer) for fig 51. The Picture Research was by Peta Hambling.

First published 1980
Second impression 1985
© text Richard I. Lawless 1980

All rights reserved. No part of this publication may be reproduced, in any form or by any means, without permission from the Publisher

Printed in Great Britain by
Anchor Brendon Ltd, Tiptree, Essex
for the Publishers Batsford Academic and
Educational, an imprint of B. T. Batsford Ltd,
4 Fitzhardinge Street, London W1H 0AH

ISBN 0 7134 2494 X

THE OTTOMAN EMPIRE AND THE TURKISH REPUBLIC

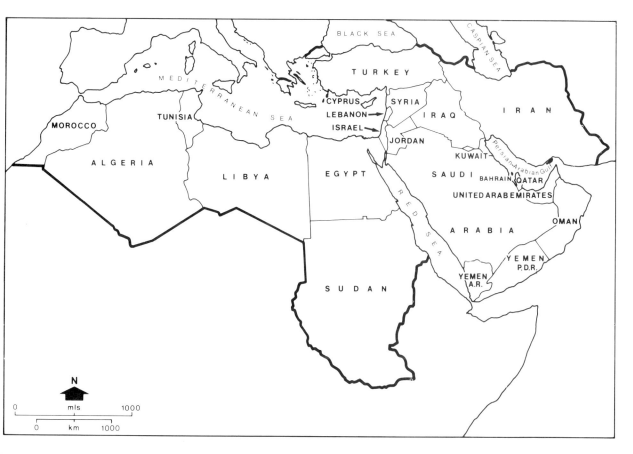

1   The Middle East: present-day political boundaries.

THE OTTOMAN BACKGROUND

At the dawn of the twentieth century much of the Middle East as we know it today still formed part of the Ottoman Empire. The Ottoman state was founded in the thirteenth century as a small principality in northwest Asia Minor by the Osmanli Turks, a small tribe from Central Asia. In the following three centuries it extended its domain by a series of remarkable conquests. Ottoman armies' advanced westwards, deep into the Balkans, destroying the remnants of the Byzantine Empire and entering the capital Constantinople, which was subsequently re-

3

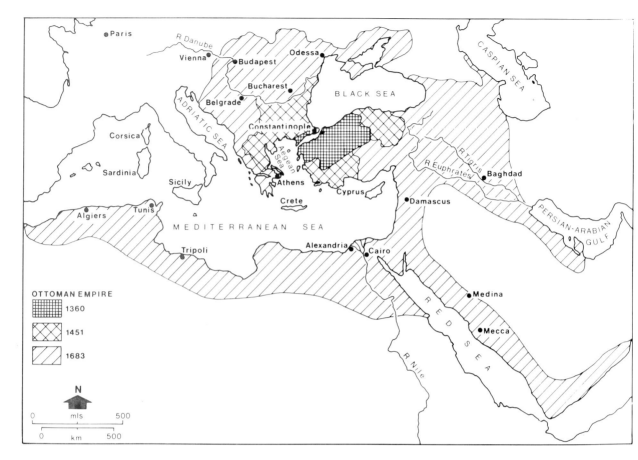

2   The expansion of the Ottoman Empire.

named Istanbul, in 1453. Asia Minor was conquered and Ottoman forces swept south to take Damascus, Baghdad and Cairo. With these conquests came the overlordship of the two holy cities of Islam: Mecca and Medina in Arabia. Turkish naval forces took Tripoli, Tunis and Algiers from Spain, and thereby established a tenuous control over the North African coastlands. In the east, the Ottoman armies advanced into Persia (now Iran), but failed to crush the new, centralized monarchy of the Safavids, then at the peak of their power, because the high plateau of Iran posed new problems of logistics and called for new and unfamiliar fighting techniques. In the far west, Morocco likewise was protected by the imposing barrier of the high Atlas mountains and did not succumb to Turkish arms. By the end of the seventeenth century the Ottoman Empire had reached the limits of its expansion. The turning point came in 1683 when the Sultan's army failed to take Vienna. From then on the Empire entered a long period of decline becoming in the memorable words of Tsar

Nicholas I of Russia "the Sick Man of Europe", until its final disintegration amid the upheavals of the First World War.

At its height, however, the Ottoman Empire had few rivals and was at the same time both feared and respected in Europe. The Ottoman military force was the best organized, and the most modern in its technology, commissariat and treatment of its troops, while Ottoman society was modernist and tolerant, compared with other societies of contemporary Europe. Though the ruling institution was Islam, the various groups of non-Muslims, Christians and Jews, had their own communal organizations known as *millets*, under their Patriarchs or Chief Rabbi. Members of each millet were free to practise their own faith and to retain their institutions, laws and traditions, under the direction of their religious leaders. By allowing this freedom the Ottoman Sultan was able to exploit the wealth produced by all his subjects, with the least possible resistance or friction. The different races and religions within the multi-national empire — Turks, Arabs, Kurds, Slavs and Greeks, Muslims, Christians and Jews — remained apart and distinct; they did not merge into an organic society. The Ottoman ruling class, the officials who administered the Empire's far-flung territories, and the soldiers of the standing army, the *janissaries*, were all slaves of the Sultan. Recruited exclusively at the outset from Christian families, they were taken as young boys to Istanbul, where they were converted to Islam and carefully trained for their future positions. The Turkish word for slave, *kul*, was regarded not as an insult but as a badge to be worn with pride.

The Ottoman systems of military organization, civil administration, taxation and land tenure were all geared to the needs of a society which was expanding by conquest and colonizing new lands. But in 1683 the period of military expansion came to an end. After humiliating defeats by the now more powerful Christian powers, Austria and Russia, the Sultan was compelled to cede extensive territories in the Balkans and Crimea. As a result, the Ottoman systems broke down and the Turks never succeeded in adopting new forms to suit the changed conditions.

At the same time, voyages of discovery, the circumnavigation of Africa, and the establishment of Europeans on the coast of India and the Persian-Arab Gulf opened up new ocean routes, and so caused the decline of the old overland trade routes. The Ottoman Empire was deprived of the greater part of her foreign commerce and the Eastern Mediterranean became an economic backwater. The Ottomans did not take part in or respond effectively to the technological advances which took place in Europe during this period and their agriculture, industry and transport remained backward. The finances of the Empire became chaotic, the value of its currency was in constant decline, and its once magnificent bureaucracy became corrupt and inefficient. A society once devoid of a landed aristocracy was overgrown by a caste of feudal lords who ruled the countryside in their own interest and oppressed the peasantry.

EUROPEAN IMPERIALISM
AND THE RISE OF NATIONALISM

In the nineteenth century the Ottoman Empire was further undermined by the rising power of western Europe and the material superiority of the major European powers which was expressed in rapid military, economic and social advances. There was growing European economic and political penetration of the Empire, while at the same time the western ideology of nationalism, the idea that each national group was entitled to political independence, began to subvert its subjects.

By the 1830s the *Capitulations*, a considerable body of rights, concessions and privileges which the Sultans had granted over the centuries to nationals of France, Britain, Austria-Hungary, Russia, Italy and Germany, had enabled foreigners to gain a stranglehold over much of the economic life of the Empire, over its finances, transportation and other services. Economic penetration was accompanied by the increasing political influence of the European powers in the Ottoman provinces. Indeed, only the intensive rivalry between the interested powers, the same rivalry which sparked off the Crimean War, prevented the partition of the Empire.

As in the case of other multi-national empires in modern times, one of the key agents in the final breakup of the Ottoman state was nationalism. This explosive idea found particularly fertile soil among the Empire's Christian subjects in the Balkans. They were actively supported and encouraged in their claims by the European powers. By the early twentieth century the rising tide of nationalism, culminating in the disastrous Balkan War of 1912, had deprived the Ottoman Empire of almost all its valuable European possessions and given independence to the Greeks, Serbs and Bulgars.

Nationalist stirrings also appeared in the Asian and African provinces of the Empire, but the aspirations of their inhabitants were to remain unfulfilled. Indeed, by the beginning of the twentieth century some of these areas had already fallen under direct European control. After Napoleon's dramatic if ill-fated invasion of Egypt in 1798, France in 1830, under the restored Bourbons, had succeeded in occupying Algiers, still nominally under Turkish suzerainty; and from here, as the century progressed, the rest of the province, stretching deep into the Sahara, was gradually brought under French military control. After the unification of Italy, France's fear of Italian imperial ambitions prompted her in 1881 to invade and declare a protectorate over neighbouring Tunisia. In both Algeria and Tunisia the French colonial authorities encouraged European settlement and the colonization of the most fertile agricultural lands. At the same time France was actively extending her cultural and economic influence in Lebanon, Syria and Palestine, although her efforts to establish a protectorate over the Maronite Christians in the early 1860s was defeated by Britain.

In 1882 the British occupied Egypt, a province which had been bankrupted by the extravagant modernization schemes of successive local rulers and which was heavily in debt to the European banking system. This brought to a logical conclusion a process of European intervention and exploitation which had begun during the reign of Egypt's first modernizing ruler, Mohammed Ali (1805-48). The invasion crushed the nascent Egyptian nationalist movement and, in spite of French efforts to compel the British to evacuate, considerations of imperial strategy ensured that Britain remained and quickly acquired complete control over the Egyptian administration. Britain, now master of India and anxious to control the main lines of communication across the Middle East, part-

icularly after the opening of the Suez Canal in 1869, had occupied Aden in 1839 and Cyprus in 1878. By the beginning of the twentieth century Britain had also established her authority over the Arab shaikhdoms along the southern shores of the Persian-Arab Gulf, persuaded the shaikhs not to grant leases or concessions without Britain's agreement, and extended her influence in the Ottoman provinces of Basra and Baghdad. Russia, in spite of her defeat in the Crimean War (1854-1856), resumed her southward expansion after 1870, occupying Batum and Kars in 1878, while at the same time actively encouraging the nationalist aspirations of the Sultan's Armenian and Kurdish subjects. In 1911 Italy, thwarted by the French in Tunisia, launched an attack on Tripoli in Libya and proclaimed her sovereignty over the coastlands of Tripolitania and Cyrenaica.

Only the German Empire, which emerged as

3 A *Punch* cartoon of 1876 illustrating the attitude of the major European powers to the Ottoman Empire and their plans to partition its territories between them.

TURKEY PIE.

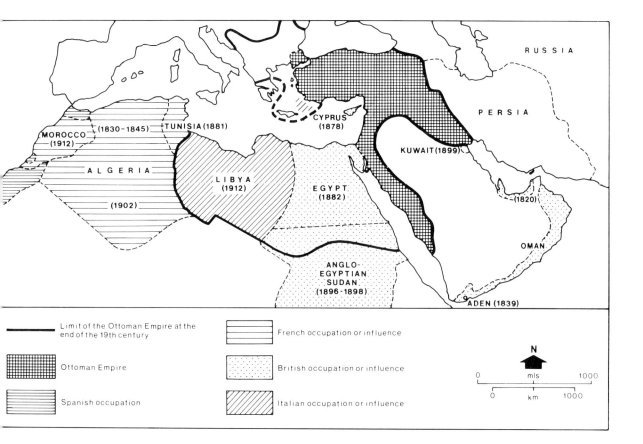

Map legend:

— Limit of the Ottoman Empire at the end of the 19th century

▦ Ottoman Empire

☰ Spanish occupation

☰ French occupation or influence

⋯ British occupation or influence

╱ Italian occupation or influence

N

0 ___ mls ___ 1000

0 ___ km ___ 1000

Map labels:

RUSSIA

PERSIA

CYPRUS (1878)

MOROCCO (1912)

(1830–1845)

TUNISIA (1881)

ALGERIA

KUWAIT (1899)

(1902)

LIBYA (1912)

EGYPT (1882)

(1820)

OMAN

ANGLO-EGYPTIAN SUDAN (1896–1898)

ADEN (1839)

4   The Middle East on the eve of the First World War.

a major European power after 1870, had an economic and political stake in the survival of the Ottoman state. While the other European powers became committed to the complete partition of the Turkish Empire, Germany, under the leadership of the flamboyant Kaiser William II, rapidly expanded its economic and financial links with the Ottoman state and was therefore anxious to protect Turkish integrity. The construction of the Berlin to Baghdad railway became a powerful symbol of the expanding German commercial and military involvement in the Ottoman Empire, and William II made well-publicized visits to Istanbul in 1889 and 1898. It was therefore to Germany that the Sultans, and after the 1908 Revolution, the Young Turks, turned for assistance in their attempts to reform and modernize the Empire's political, social and economic structure. While Britain and France, fearful of the expansionist policies of the new German state, formed the Entente Cordiale in 1904 which was extended to Russia in 1907, the Ottoman Empire was drawn irretrievably into the German orbit by her nationalist leaders.

THE 1908 REVOLUTION

In the late nineteenth century the manifest decline of the Ottoman Empire, in the face of European imperialism and technological superiority, had prompted calls for reform from Young Ottoman groups. During the early years of the twentieth century the number of revolutionary groups, working in secret for fear of the Sultan's omnipresent spies, multiplied, and by 1908 the army officers in Macedonia had become the centre of opposition. This opposition to Sultan Abdul Hamid's despotic rule was widespread among the new educated classes of government servants and young Prussian-trained military officers, who believed that the shortcomings of the Ottoman state system could not be fully overcome and the Empire saved from total collapse until the Sultan's powers were legally curbed by the introduction of a constitution of the European type.

On 21 July 1908 the Salonika branch of the Society for Union & Progress sent a telegram to the Sultan demanding the immediate restoration of the 1876 Constitution, long since in abeyance.

THE ADOPTED FATHER.

5 A *Punch* cartoon portrays the despotic Sultan Abdul Hamid who in 1908 was compelled by the Young Turks to restore the 1876 Constitution and to convene a Turkish parliament.

After some hesitation, during which he received alarming reports of rebellion, Abdul Hamid suddenly gave way. On 24 July he announced that the Constitution was once again in force and convened a Chamber of Deputies. Spontaneous demonstrations of joy broke out in many parts of the Empire at this dawning of a new era of freedom and brotherhood.

But the great hopes engendered by this revolution were almost bound to lead to disillusion and disappointment. There were two strands in the rather vaguely defined politics of what later became known as the Young Turk movement. On the one hand, the Liberals favoured some degree of decentralization and autonomy for the religious and national minorities. (Some among the Arab, Christian and other minorities supported the Young Turks initially, but it soon became apparent that a policy of decentralization was not to be pursued.) On the other hand, the Committee for Union & Progress (CUP), as the Salonika officers styled themselves, endorsed the nationalist call for greater central authority and Turkish dominance in the Empire over other races. The Liberals melted into ineffectual opposition groups, while the CUP, although remaining in the background, exerted pressure on the government and manipulated appointments.

By early 1909, after the loss of the Balkan States and troubled months of constitutional government, both Sultan and Liberals were opposed to the regime. In April 1909 the First Army Corps in Istanbul mutinied and a general rising took place, accompanied by risings across Anatolia, calling for the restoration of the Holy Law of Islam (*Sharia*). It was crushed by the arrival of reinforcements from Salonika, and the CUP took the opportunity to depose Abdul Hamid, and replace him with a new Sultan, Mehmed Resad, who dutifully installed their nominees in key palace positions.

THE RULE OF THE COMMITTEE OF UNION & PROGRESS

The CUP were now undisputed rulers of the Empire, and the martial law imposed after the mutiny continued in force until 1911. The CUP's principal concern was to save the Empire, and they embarked upon a series of centralizing and repressive measures, which were intended to improve provincial and local administration, increase revenue to the government and strengthen the state. They also carried out an energetic programme of public works in the capital and tried to westernize and modernize Ottoman society and government. These measures caused a lot of difficulties in the bureaucracy, and ill-feeling in the provinces, but what was most resented were the attempts to impose the Turkish language on Christians and non-Turkish Muslims. National and minority associations and societies were also ruthlessly repressed. The CUP's principal achievement was in the field of education, where they set up a new system of schooling, and encouraged the education of women and their entry into public life. During the First World War, when the men were largely drawn away into the army, Turkish women entered the professions and the factories, and began to achieve emancipation.

Opposition to the all-powerful Committee's rule grew, but their position was not seriously challenged until a major split appeared in their ranks in early 1911. This weakened their authority and prestige. A new party, the Liberal Union, an amalgam of almost all those in opposition to the CUP, was formed, and it drew increasing support. When the Liberal Union won a by-election at the end of 1911, the CUP sensed a threat to its position and called a general election. In April 1912, in what is known as "the big-stick election", the CUP ensured that it obtained 269 out of 275 seats in the Chamber.

The opposition was crushed. And this led to the formation of a military conspiracy of "Saviour Officers" who put the CUP out of power by threatening military revolt, upon which the government resigned. A new cabinet was formed which met with the approval of the military conspirators. But with the "Saviour Officers" busy fighting off the Italian invasion of Tripolitania, and then the attack of the Balkan Allies in October 1912, the new government was very weak, and the CUP made its plans to seize back power by force.

THE RULE OF THE TRIUMVIRATE

In January 1913 a group of CUP members, led by Enver Pasha, forced their way into the cabinet room, shooting dead the Minister of War and compelling the Grand Vezir to resign. The CUP was now firmly in power. They proceeded to remove every trace of the freedom and democracy for which they had once fought. From 1913 until 1918 Turkey was ruled by a military oligarchy dominated by three men.

Enver Pasha, a man of humble origins, graduated from the War College of Istanbul, served as military attaché in Berlin after the Revolution, and became Minister of War in 1913. He was a popular officer and clever politician and in 1914 he married an Ottoman Princess. He, more than any other single person, brought Turkey into the First World War, signing a secret treaty with Germany in 1914.

1916 the Arab Revolt was declared, and when the armistice ending the First World War was signed in 1918, the Empire was effectively broken up. The triumvirs fled across the Black Sea in a German warship and were court-martialled *in absentia*. Talât and Djemal were both assassinated by Armenians, bent on avenging the massacres of 1915. Enver Pasha fled eventually to Uzbekistan and attempted to lead the local nationalists against the Bolsheviks. He was killed in a battle with Soviet troops.

ATATÜRK AND THE CREATION OF THE MODERN TURKISH REPUBLIC

The "Sick Man of Europe" perished in the First World War. Under the leadership of the Young Turks, the Ottoman Empire had entered the war recklessly, and although the Turkish armies put up a spirited resistance — the defence of Gallipoli alone cost the Turks 55,000 killed and 100,000 wounded — they could not avert defeat. The Arab provinces of the Empire were occupied by Allied forces and only Anatolia, Eastern Thrace and the capital Istanbul were left under Ottoman control when the armistice was signed in October 1918. The victorious Allies were poised to partition the very heartland of the Empire and deny the Turks the two supreme modern rights of self-determination and majority rule. They failed, largely through the efforts of one man, Mustafa Kemal, the founder of the modern Turkish Republic, who later took the name Atatürk, meaning father of the Turks.

Mustafa Kemal was born in Salonika in 1881, the son of a minor Ottoman civil servant. Like many other Turks of lower-middle-class background, he chose the army for his career. In 1906 he founded a secret opposition group in Salonika and took part in the work of the Committee of Union and Progress. But his relations with the Young Turks were far from cordial and after the 1908 Revolution he abandoned politics and devoted himself to his military career. He achieved rapid promotion and by 1918 he was the only remaining victorious general in Turkey. His military successes made him a popular hero and allowed him later to take undisputed command of all the Turkish nationalist forces which resisted the envisaged partition of their country. Mustafa

6 Enver Pasha, one of the leaders of the Young Turks. Together with Djemal and Talât Pasha, he ruled Turkey from 1913 to 1918.

Djemal Pasha came from a military family, and was also a graduate of the War College. A cool and professional military officer, he became notorious for his ruthlessness as Turkish commander in Syria during the First World War.

Talât Pasha was from a poor family. As Chief Secretary of the directorate of the telegraph office at Salonika, he rendered good service to the Young Turks. He later rose rapidly in the CUP and in 1916 became Grand Vezir. He was a shrewd politician and unquestionably the ablest of the three triumvirs.

Under their rule, state control became tighter and more powerful and repressive. In 1914 they brought Turkey into the war on the side of Germany, with whom they had close political and economic links, fearing partition at the hands of the western Europeans and Russia. In 1915 the large Armenian communities of Anatolia were deported, with such brutality that few survived, on the grounds that they might intrigue with Russia against the state. But in

10

Kemal created the Turkish Republic. He won its territory, chose and built its capital, shaped its institutions, developed its alphabet and even its language, and set it on a road of his choosing. His genius was the embodiment of the aspirations of educated Turks of his background and generation.

Following the armistice of 1918 the Sultan, who had assumed power after the fall of the Young Turks, believed that some form of Allied protectorate was inevitable. The country was shattered, impoverished, depopulated and demoralized. The Turkish people, beaten and dispirited, seemed ready to accept almost anything that the victors chose to impose on them. Allied forces were even threatening the Turkish provinces themselves. French troops advanced from Syria into Cilicia and the Adana district. British forces occupied the Dardanelles, Samsun, Ayntab and other strategic points as well as the whole length of the Anatolian railway. An Allied military administration was set up in Istanbul, and Italian troops landed at Antalya to take possession of some of the areas assigned to them by the secret wartime agreements of the Allies. In August 1920 the Sultan's government was obliged to give in to the Allies' united demands, set forth in the Treaty of Sèvres. This left to Turkey nothing but Istanbul and a corner of Asia Minor. Turkish subjection appeared complete. But not quite. In May 1919, under cover of Allied warships, a Greek army landed at Izmir. The Turkish reaction was violent and instantaneous. The Greeks made it clear from the outset that they had come, not for a temporary occupation, but to annex the land for good, to incorporate Western Anatolia into a greater Greece and restore the glories of the Byzantine Empire. The thrust of a former subject people into the very heart of Turkish Anatolia was a humiliation almost beyond endurance. The Turks were ready to rise against the invader in a war of liberation — their chosen leader, Mustafa Kemal.

Mustafa Kemal had refused to accept the defeatist attitude of the Sultan's government before the Allied threat, and since 1918 had been actively organizing resistance movements in the Anatolian interior. Ordered by the Sultan to supervise the disarmament and demobilization of the remaining Ottoman forces, he set to work instead establishing links between existing resistance groups and forming new ones. He organized an "Association for the Defence of the Rights of Anatolia and Rumelia", which demanded the preservation of territorial integrity and national independence. Ankara, a small Anatolian town later to be the capital of the new Turkish Republic, became the headquarters of the Grand National Assembly which embodied the nationalist resistance.

At first, the Turkish forces, hopelessly outmatched in numbers and equipment, were badly defeated by the Greeks in campaigns during 1920 and 1921. But at the end of August 1921 a Turkish army, under the personal command of Mustafa Kemal, won a decisive victory over the Greeks at Sakarya. The effects of Sakarya were considerable. The nationalists were now acknowledged internationally as a force to be reckoned with, and by some as the real government of Turkey. The Soviet Union had already signed an agreement with them in March 1921, fixing the frontier and establishing friendly relations; the French now did the same. A new Franco-Turkish Treaty was signed with the nationalists. It drew up a new Turco-Syrian frontier which was far more favourable to Turkey than the one established in the Treaty of Sèvres and it provided for the French evacuation of Cilicia. The Italians also withdrew from their zone in southern Anatolia.

In August 1922 the third and final phase of the Greco-Turkish war began, in which the Turks drove back the Greeks and reoccupied Izmir. The reconquest of Anatolia was complete and at the end of 1922 the Allied governments agreed to restore Turkish sovereignty in Istanbul, the Straits and Eastern Thrace. A peace conference at Lausanne in November 1922 re-established complete and undivided Turkish sovereignty in almost all the territory included in the present-day Turkish Republic. In this way Turkey rose from her own ruins and rejected the dictated peace imposed on her by the victorious Allies.

Now that the military battle had been won, Mustafa Kemal renounced all foreign ambitions. He quickly made peace with the Greeks, settling ancient disputes between them by the brutal but effective method of an exchange of populations. The rest of his life was devoted to the daunting and unglamorous task of reconstructing and reshaping his devastated country. In a speech in 1923 he warned the Turkish people:

The successes which our army has gained up to now cannot be regarded as having achieved the real salvation of our country. These victories have only prepared the ground for

7 Cheering Turks surround the Turkish flag to celebrate the victory of the Turkish army over the Greeks and the reoccupation of Izmir (Smyrna) in 1922.

our future victories. Let us not be puffed up with military victories. Let us rather prepare for new victories in science and economics.

It was in this task that Mustafa Kemal showed his true greatness.

THE ATATÜRK REVOLUTION

The first problem to be solved was a political one: what should be the form and structure of the Turkish state? The Ottoman Sultanate had lingered on through the traumatic events of the nationalist struggle. But, in spite of its immense prestige and authority, inherited over five centuries, it was abolished in 1922. The last Sultan, Mehmed V1 Vahideddin, fled from Istanbul on board a British battleship. The Grand National Assembly proclaimed a republic and elected Mustafa Kemal to be its first president. Mustafa Kemal then organized his supporters in a solid front under the name of the People's Party (later the Republican People's Party). This was to be Turkey's sole political party and a school for the political education of the Turkish people. Ankara was declared the seat of government of the new republic in place of Istanbul. Istanbul was too intimately associated with Turkey's imperial past — the memory of which Mustafa Kemal was determined to erase.

Mustafa Kemal fervently believed that Turkey must become part of the modern world in order to survive, and modernization for him meant westernization. He saw the Islamic religious establishment, with its elaborate hierarchical organization, as the major obstacle to the progress of westernization and was determined to sweep it away. The office of Caliphate, the spiritual leadership of the Muslim world, which had been held by successive Ottoman Sultans, was now abolished. So were the separate religious schools and colleges, and the courts which administered the Holy Law. When the Kurds rebelled in 1925, led by dervish shaikhs, Mustafa Kemal swiftly crushed the uprising and used the opportunity to suppress dervish orders throughout the country, closing their convents, disbanding their associations and banning their meetings and ceremonies. At the same time the Assembly banned the wearing of the fez

12

(tarboosh) and turbans, forms of headgear with distinctly Islamic associations. All civil servants were required to wear "the costume common to the civilized nations of the world — that is the western suit and hat". New codes of law based on European models replaced the Holy Law of Islam, completing the work of secularization. In April 1928 the Assembly deleted from the Constitution the reference to Islam as the official religion of the state. Then in November 1928 use of the Arabic alphabet, the final badge of Muslim identity, was banned and an adapted

form of the Latin alphabet was introduced as the official Turkish script. Mustafa Kemal himself set out on a tour of the country with blackboard and easel, to teach the people to read and write the new script.

Economic matters dominated the last ten years of Mustafa Kemal's life. With a legacy of underdevelopment, a lack of skills and capital, and the devastation of war, Turkey needed an economic expansion that would develop her resources, create new industries and raise the standard of living of the people. His original economic policy was to encourage Turkish private enterprise within a mixed and largely state-regulated economy. But the main economic enterprises in the country had been foreign-owned and these were nationalized one by one. The railways, the country's only important coalfield at Zonguldak on the Black

8 Turkish refugees from Greece being helped off the boat which had arrived in Turkey in October 1923. After the Treaty of Lausanne in July 1923 all the Greeks in Turkey, apart from the reduced community in Istanbul, were expelled in exchange for the smaller number of Turks in Greece.

9　Mustafa Kemal (centre), later known as Atatürk, the founder of the modern Turkish Republic, arriving in Istanbul, 1928. He is surrounded by Ministers and General Officers.

Sea, the ports and public services all came to be run by the state. This policy of nationalization was accentuated after the world economic crisis of 1929, when state capitalism or *étatism* became official dogma. Major efforts were made to extend the railway network and in 1933 the first Turkish five year plan was prepared for the expansion of Turkish industry. The first modern textile factories were built with Soviet aid, and Turkey's first steel mill was established with British assistance. However, agriculture, the mainstay of the country's economy, was neglected and agricultural production did not rise. While the institutions of the country were given a modern look, the economy from which they drew their strength remained backward.

Mustafa Kemal, who had assumed the name Kemal Atatürk in 1934, died suddenly in November 1938 at the age of 57. Opinions are divided on the success and wisdom of many of his policies. Some insist that his reforms affected only the towns and the urban classes and brought little change to the peasant majority; others felt that his policies produced too violent a break with the nation's religious and cultural traditions. Yet it is indisputable that, at the darkest moment in their history, Atatürk brought new life and hope to the Turkish people and restored their energies and self-respect. Indeed, one of his much quoted slogans was: "Turk, work, be proud, be confident".

TURKEY'S STRUGGLE TOWARDS DEMOCRACY

The day after Atatürk's death the Grand National Assembly unanimously voted Ismet Inönü, his lifelong friend and closest collaborator, to be his successor. Inönü continued to rule Turkey as a one-party state during the difficult years of the Second World War. When the war ended in 1945 some members of the ruling Republican People's Party were criticizing more and more the strict authoritarian style of government inherited from the Atatürk era and the repressive measures adopted during the war years. They demanded the relaxation of the state's tight control over the economy, greater incentives for private enterprise, increased rural development and less hostile policy on the role of religion in public life. Against this background Inönü decided upon a momentous change of course — announcing in November 1945 that he favoured the creation of an opposition party. The Democrat Party was founded in January 1946 by four former members of the RPP — Adnan Menderes, Mehmed Fuad Köprülü, Celal Bayar and Refik Koraltan. It won 62 of the 465 parliamentary seats in the general election of 1946, and achieved a landslide victory with 408 seats in 1950. With Adnan Menderes as her new Prime Minister, Turkey had transferred peacefully to a competitive party system.

The Democrat Party programme of 1950 achieved some startling successes during the "Democrat decade" which followed. Per capita income had hardly increased at all in real terms between 1938 and 1950, but during the next ten years it rose by nearly 40 per cent. Cereal production increased by leaps and bounds, helped by favourable climatic conditions during the early fifties, huge injections of American aid and greater use of tractors bringing changes to Turkish rural life which none of the earlier reforms had achieved. Industrial development in both the state and private sectors also expanded rapidly. Incentives replaced directives and, instead of relying on government decrees, the Democrats concentrated on creating economic inducements which vastly broadened the scope of the Atatürk revolution.

THE ARMY INTERVENES

While everything seemed to go right for the Democrats between 1950 and 1954, in the late 1950s most things went wrong. There were mounting foreign debts, lack of economic planning and chronic inflation. Civil servants and army officers on fixed salaries were among those most seriously affected by the sharp increase in the cost of living between 1955 and 1960, and they represented the two groups particularly hostile to the Menderes government. At the same time the Republican People's Party, now in opposition, feared that the Democrats were planning to convert their parliamentary majority into a political monopoly. This fear appeared to be justified when the restrictive Press Law of 1954 was followed a year later by the arrest of the RPP's Secretary General. Although the Democrat Party retained their majority in the

1957 elections, there were widespread suspicions that the elections had been rigged. Misgivings increased during early 1960 as the government attempted to interfere with Inönü's freedom of movement and established a "Committee to Investigate the Republican People's Party and a Section of the Press", with complete powers of search and arrest.

On 28 April 1960 students in Istanbul demonstrated against the Menderes government. The universities had for some time been the focus of anti-government feeling and in consequence had found their liberties curtailed. Troops were called on to fire, and martial law was declared in Ankara and Istanbul. The military were then faced with a choice of either supporting Menderes or bringing him down. On 27 May 1960 the army chiefs, led by General Cemal Gürsel, the Commander of Land Forces, arrested the entire Cabinet and DP Parliamentary group, replacing them with a 38-man National Unity Committee drawn from their own ranks and a non-party caretaker cabinet. The leaders of the Democrats were charged with violating the Constitution and three of them, the Prime Minister, Adnan Menderes, the Foreign Minister, Fatin Rüstü Zorlu, and the Minister of Finance, Hasan Polatkan, were hanged in September 1961 after a long political trial.

The military had carried out their coup with remarkable efficiency, but they were not agreed about the ultimate purpose of their intervention. An important group of junior officers believed that a competitive party system was premature and favoured a long-term military regime. The majority of senior officers, on the other hand, favoured a speedy return to civilian government and in the end their views prevailed. Just over a year after the coup the military carried out its promise and handed over power to the civilians. This was after the introduction of a new Constitution and the organization of new general elections under a revised electoral law.

The 1961 elections left the RPP as the largest party in power. But it had no overall majority and was seriously challenged by the newly formed Justice Party, which claimed to be the heir of the now outlawed Democrat Party. For the next four years Turkey was ruled by fragile coalitions under the veteran politican Inönü. During this time there were two attempted *coups d'état* by army radicals. Then, in the October 1965 elections, the Justice Party under their new leader Süleyman Demirel won a workable parliamentary majority, which they renewed in

10 The Turkish army takes over a government building in Istanbul during the military coup d'état in 1960.

1969. However, Demirel's government was plagued by defections from his party and, after 1968, by the mounting level of violence as right- and left-wing student groups and trade unionists clashed in street battles. Once again the army generals intervened. In March 1971 they overthrew Demirel's government and replaced it with an above-party coalition, calling for a "strong and credible government which would put an end to the present anarchic situation". Terrorists were rounded up, together with many suspected of Marxist sympathies. Evidence that torture was used against at least some of those arrested caused a serious setback for Turkey's reputation in western Europe. Yet, unlike 1960, the army declined to take over outright and there was a return to normal civilian party politics in October 1973.

THE CYPRUS CRISIS

After Cyprus gained independence from Britain in 1960 there was a rapid deterioration in relations between the Turkish Cypriot community, who make up between 18 and 20 per cent of the island's population, and the Greek Cypriot majority, led by the President, Archbishop Makarios. The Turkish Cypriots were virtually excluded from any effective role in the central government of Cyprus, and when Makarios built up his own army, the National Guard, officered by Greeks from the mainland, the Turkish Cypriots retaliated by forming their own militias to protect the scattered enclaves where they were now hemmed in. Clashes between the two communities almost provoked Turkish intervention in support of the Turkish Cypriots in 1964 and again in 1967. Finally Turkey did take military action in 1974. On 15 July 1974 the Greek junta in Athens used the National Guard to oust President Makarios and replace him with Nikos Sampson. Sampson was notorious for his ruthless killings during the EOKA campaign against the British and for his hatred of the Turks, and so Turkey now took action to protect the Turks in Cyprus. The government of Bülent Ecevit, who had succeeded the ageing Inönü as leader of the RPP, ordered Turkish troops into Cyprus on 20 July 1974. A peace conference organized in Geneva in August between Britain, Greece and Turkey failed to achieve a settlement and Turkish forces made a second advance. They

16

occupied the whole of Cyprus north of a line running from Morphou through Nicosia to Famagusta which is named the "Attila line". In February 1975 the Turkish Cypriots unilaterally declared a "Turkish Federated State of Cyprus" in the northern part of the island.

The Cyprus crisis brought about important changes in Turkey's international relations. The powerful Greek lobby in the United States Congress forced through an arms embargo on Turkey, whose armed forces are largely American equipped. In retaliation, in July 1975, the Turks took over America's numerous radar and military bases in Turkey. There were fears that Turkey might withdraw from NATO and there was anxiety in the west when Ecevit began to flirt with the Soviet Union.

At home, the Cyprus landings greatly strengthened Ecevit's popularity, but they also contributed to the collapse of his fragile and unnatural coalition with the pro-Islamic National Salvation Party. Ecevit's resignation in September 1974 plunged Turkish political life once again into a state of confusion.

POLITICAL MURDER AND THE CRISIS OF TURKISH DEMOCRACY

During the 1960s and 1970s the growth of a Turkish working class and the mounting class-consciousness of the electorate forced the major political parties to redefine their positions. By the early 1970s the RPP, converted by Ecevit to a programme of moderate socialism, had emerged as the party of the moderate left; the Justice Party as that of the moderate right. But neither enjoyed an overall majority in parliament. Consequently they have been forced to govern by forming precarious coalitions with one or more of the smaller parties represented in the Assembly. In March 1975 Demirel returned to power, leading a weak right-wing coalition. It survived until 1977, only by avoiding taking any radical measures which

11 Turkish reinforcements landing near Kyrenia during the Turkish invasion of Cyprus in 1974.

might upset the cooperation between the members. This prevented them from tackling urgent problems of mounting unemployment, rising inflation and crippling foreign debts. Economic paralysis was accompanied by increasing political violence throughout Turkey, especially in the universities, between right- and left-wing groups. Progress towards a settlement of the Cyprus question was also hampered by the weakness of the coalition.

Ecevit, who replaced Demirel in January 1978 at the head of yet another coalition government, also failed to reform the economy, contain runaway inflation or stamp out the mounting political violence which endangered the very existence of democracy. Pressure of economic crises, mounting political killings by extreme right and left, inter-communal riots like those which claimed 100 lives at Maras in December 1978 and growing separatist movements among Kurds and other minorities seriously threatened the security of the Turkish state and the survival

12 Turks accused of being members of a left-wing terrorist organization, together with their weapons. Mounting violence by both the extreme right and left characterized Turkish politics during the 1970s.

of its democratic, western and secular institutions. The government was compelled to place much of the country, including the two major cities, Istanbul and Ankara, under martial law.

The political instability of the 1970s deprived the country of guidance, discipline and direction. Parliament failed to rally round. The parties were too hostile to unite even under the gravest circumstances, yet many members crossed the floor for personal financial and political gain, badly tarnishing the image of democracy in the eyes of the people. One party, the neo-fascist National Action, went so far as to form its own force of well-trained and well-armed commandos known as "grey wolves" who were implicated in the Maras massacre. The prospect of a new military intervention remained a real possibility.

18

YOUNG HISTORIAN

A

1 Outline the main factors contributing to the decline of the Ottoman Empire.
2 Discuss the development of nationalism in the Ottoman Empire in the nineteenth century.
3 Write short explanations of the following: (a) nationalism; (b) millet; (c) janissaries.
4 Write a paragraph on how each of the following countries expanded into the Ottoman Empire: (a) Britain; (b) Russia; (c) France; (d) Italy.
5 What were the differences between the Liberals and the Committee for Union & Progress?
6 Summarize the policies followed by the Committee of Union & Progress and why they were so unpopular.
7 Write short biographies of the leaders of the Triumvirate.
8 What were the main aims of Mustafa Kemal's policies of modernization?
9 Explain why the military intervened in Turkish politics in 1960 and again in 1976.

B

1 Imagine you are a member of the Young Turk movement, writing a letter to your parents in which you explain why you have joined the opposition movement.
2 Write a newspaper obituary for Mustafa Kemal.

C

1 Write the newspaper headlines which might have appeared above reports on: (a) the 1908 Revolution; (b) the victory at Sakarya — August 1921; (c) the election of Mustafa Kemal as the first Turkish President; (d) the victory of the Democrat party in the election of 1950; (e) student riots in Ankara and Istanbul 1960; (f) the declaration of martial law in Istanbul and Ankara in 1978.

D

1 Draw a map showing the extent of the Ottoman Empire at its peak.
2 Plot the path of the "Attila line" on Cyprus.

IRAN – FROM EMPIRE TO ISLAMIC REPUBLIC

IRAN AT THE TURN OF THE CENTURY

At the beginning of the twentieth century Iran, or Persia as it was known until 1934, was still ruled by the Qajar dynasty who had held power since the late eighteenth century. The people were discontented with the government of the Shah, especially because of the extravagant life-style of the ruler and his court. Government was very weak, and while the Shah held absolute power, much of the work was done by the Grand Vezir. Governorships of provinces were sold to the highest bidder, and so the peasantry were at the mercy of corrupt landlords and minor officials. Law courts were controlled by the religious teachers, the Mullahs, and bribing courts for a favourable verdict was common.

Some progress had been made in modernizing the country — the printing press became common after 1823 and the first telegraph line was laid in 1864. Iranian intellectuals, like their Ottoman counterparts, admired and approved the introduction of advanced European technical skills. What they did object to were the vast economic concessions the Shah granted to Europeans, the terms of which were usually unfavourable to Iran. In 1889, for example, Baron Julius de Reuter (a naturalized British subject then working for the Imperial Bank of Russia) was given the sole right of issuing bank notes in Iran and total control of all mining enterprises. In the same year Britain was granted the concession to control production, preparation and sale of tobacco. In 1901 an Englishman by the name of William Knox D'Arcy obtained the rights of oil exploration and production throughout Iran, in return for

£20,000 in cash and a promise of a further £20,000 in shares. This later formed the basis for the Anglo-Persian Oil Company.

THE GROWTH OF NATIONALISM

The Shah on the throne at the turn of the century, Muzaffar-al-Din, continued the extravagant ways of his predecessors, driving the country to the verge of bankruptcy. In 1900 and 1902 he was forced to raise two further loans, this time from the Russian Bank de Prêts, and much of this money was used to finance his visit to Europe. The corruption of the court, and the great resentment against increasing foreign influence led to popular demands for constitutional reform.

In 1905 two external events encouraged the nationalists in Iran. The first was the defeat in war of the hitherto invincible Russian army by the Japanese — the first time an Asian state had defeated a major European power. The second was the 1905 revolution in Russia. When it failed, many of the revolutionaries fled to Iran where they encouraged the spread of revolutionary ideas.

Two leaders of the constitutional movement emerged: Jamal al-Din al-Afghani and Malkon Khan. In 1905-06 the resistance movement in Iran grew, and gained further popularity when its leaders took refuge in the mosques in Tehran and Qom, demanding the dismissal of the Grand Vezir Ayn-al-Dawla. This action paralysed the economic life of the capital, and the Shah was forced to agree to dismiss the Grand Vezir, to

establish courts of justice, and to incur no more
foreign debts.

However, the Shah broke his promise and in
1906 all the Tehran clergy withdrew to the
mosque, an act of defiance against the Shah,
signifying a withdrawal from civic life, while
12,000 Tehranis took refuge in the grounds of
the British Legation. The nationalists demanded
a Majlis, or Parliament. In view of the mounting
unrest, the Shah agreed to the demands of the
constitutionalists, dismissing Ayn-al-Dawla as
Grand Vezir, and signing a proclamation which
authorized the formation of a Majlis. The
election took place, and the Majlis was convened
on 7 October 1906.

CONSTITUTIONAL ADMINISTRATION
1908-1914

Muzaffar Shah died in 1907 and his successor,
Mohammed II, tried to disband the Majlis and
replace it with a council of his own. He caused
further resentment when he reinstated al-Dawla
as Grand Vezir, and dismissed the more liberal
Mirza Nasr Khan who had replaced him.

Worried by what they saw as the growing
influence of Germany in Iran, Britain and Russia
in August 1907 divided Iran into three zones for
commercial purposes: the north for Russia, the
southeast for Britain, and a neutral zone

**13   British and Russian spheres of influence as laid
down in 1907.**

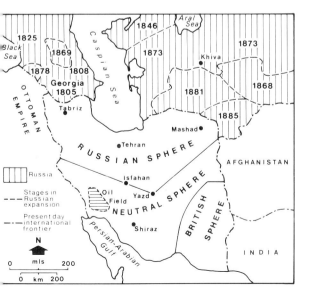

AS BETWEEN FRIENDS.

**14   A _Punch_ cartoon of 1911 drawing attention to
continued British and Russian rivalry in Iran (Persia)
after Britain and Russia had divided the country into
three zones for commercial purposes in 1907.**

between them. This action encouraged nationalist feeling in Iran against the influence of out-
siders.

Two main political movements emerged in
Iran, the Royalists, who supported the Shah,
and the Constitutionalists. The Constitutionalists formed the liberal opposition to the Shah's
rule; they had been encouraged by the successful
revolution in 1908 in the neighbouring Ottoman
Empire. The Russians supported the Shah, and
in 1908 when a bomb was thrown at his car, the
Russians formed and trained the Cossack
Brigade to protect him. The Cossack Brigade
were responsible for bombing the Majlis in
Tehran in 1908, killing its leaders. The British
ambassador, on the other hand, advised the Shah
to yield to the demands of the Constitutionalists.

By 1909 civil war had broken out in the
provinces. The Bakhtiari tribe from the north,
with an ambitious leader, marched on Tehran
and occupied the city. The Shah retreated to the
Russian embassy in Tehran, abdicated and fled
to Russia. Russian forces invaded the northern
province of Iran in April 1909 and occupied the
major city of Tabriz.

The eleven year old Ahmad Mirza was made Shah, and Nasr al-Mulk, the head of the Qajar tribe, was appointed regent. A new Majlis was convened, but Russian encroachment continued. The Russians maintained their troops in Tabriz and encouraged the ex-Shah in his efforts to regain the throne when he landed near Asterabad in 1911. In an attempt to balance between Britain and Russia, the Majlis asked the United States of America to send advisers. William Morgan Shuster was made Treasurer General in Iran until 1911. He was employed to get the Iranian finances into some kind of order. The Majlis was also sympathetic to Germany, realizing that if she won the war in Europe, Iran would stand a better chance of ridding herself of British and Russian influence.

THE FIRST WORLD WAR AND ITS EFFECTS ON IRAN

When Britain and Russia declared war on Ottoman Turkey in November 1914, Iran declared her neutrality. In the south and east of Iran, British intervention increased as the work of German political agents encouraged tribal and nationalist disorders. Russia launched major offensives into Turkey from Iranian territory, while Turks attacked Russia through the Zagros Mountains in Iran. With the Iranian central government being so weak, tribal leaders took this as an opportunity to assert their independence.

By 1915 the Anglo-Russian agreement of 1907 was transformed into a virtual partition. The Russians gained total liberty of action in the north, and the neutral zone went to the British.

THE REVOLUTION IN RUSSIA

With the end of the First World War and the 1917 revolution in Russia, the political scenario in the area changed. The Soviet leadership was preoccupied with the domestic political scene after the revolution and wanted Russian troops to withdraw quickly from Iranian territory. As the Russians withdrew, the way now lay open for the Germans to march through northern Iran towards Afghanistan and India. But, in fact,

both Germany and Turkey were too preoccupied elsewhere to take advantage of the situation in the northern provinces of Iran, and British troops were able to maintain control.

Britain was by now the dominant power in Iran. In 1919 she negotiated an agreement by which British advisers were to join Iranian government departments. Customs tariffs were reorganized in Britain's favour, and roads and railways were to be constructed with British aid. The Majlis refused to ratify this agreement however, and British advisers were replaced by Americans.

THE RISE OF REZA SHAH

Against the background of weak central government and increasing foreign influence, Sayyid Zia al-Din Tabatabai, a journalist and politician, organized a bloodless coup with the backing of a commanding officer of the Persian Cossack Brigade — Reza Khan. This took place in February 1921. Tabatabai was made Prime Minister, and Reza Khan appointed Commander-in-Chief of the armed forces. The Anglo-Persian agreement was denounced, Tabatabai resigned as Prime Minister, and Reza Khan was left in control. He was made Prime Minister in 1923, whereupon he assembled the Majlis.

The economic situation in the country had improved slightly with the help of American advisers, notably Arthur G. Millspaugh, and with the revenue from the Anglo-Persian Oil Company (APOC), later to become British Petroleum (BP).

In February 1925 the Majlis agreed to make Reza Khan Commander-in-Chief of the Iranian armed forces for life. Then, on 31 October the Majlis declared the Qajar dynasty deposed. Reza Khan was proclaimed the new Shah on 12 December 1925 and crowned Reza Shah Pahlavi (meaning "True Persian") on 25 April 1926.

THE REIGN OF REZA SHAH

The reign of Reza Shah was marked by two principal trends. One was a policy of modernization along western lines similar to that of

5   Reza Shah Pahlavi.

Reza Shah introduced a policy of compulsory settlement of nomadic tribesmen which prevented their seasonal migration. This policy was not always applied sensibly where stock-breeding was the natural means of existence, and it often caused severe hardship. Tribal rebellions against the policy resulted, but these were ruthlessly crushed, and the leaders were held as hostages in Tehran.

The second main trend discernible in the reign of Reza Shah was a determined attempt to free Iran from British and Russian influence and to establish a strong central government. In 1926 the Majlis passed a universal conscription law which meant that there was a regular army of 40,000 supporting the government. In 1932 Reza Shah's government objected to the agreement under which the Anglo-Persian Oil Company operated. A new agreement was formulated in 1933 which gave Iran a larger share of the profits. At the same time German influence in Iran grew in the 1930s, as Germany supplied Iran with heavy machinery, technicians and advisers. This increase in German influence encouraged Russia, Britain and America to form a Tripartite Agreement in 1940. During the Second World War Iran declared her neutrality, but even so she turned down a request by the Allies to expel German nationals from her territory, and this led to Russian and British forces occupying Iran in August 1941.

Reza Shah's autocratic methods caused resentment among many Constitutional supporters. His ministers often did not tell him of public opinion about his policies. In his latter years he became greedy, and much of the national wealth went into his own pocket. By the end of his reign much of his popularity had gone and the considerable progress made in the earlier years was forgotten.

On 16 September 1941 under Allied pressure Reza Shah abdicated in favour of his son, Muhammad Reza. At first the new Shah's position was weak. A nationalist government formed by Dr Musaddiq in 1951 nationalized the Iranian oil industry and forced the Shah into a brief exile. But he returned after a coup organized by the army and the American CIA had toppled Musaddiq in 1953. After his return the young Shah, who had become well-known as an international playboy, began to take a more active interest in the country's administration. Eventually he succeeded in concentrating all power in his own hands, ruling in an even more autocratic manner than his father.

Atatürk in Turkey. For example, he introduced the French system of justice, so stopping the influence of religious courts in civil matters. In 1928 a decree was passed which made the wearing of native costume illegal for towns-women, peasants and tribesmen. In 1936 he outlawed the veil for women, and took some religious-owned land back in an attempt to lessen the grip which the clergy had on the people. Reza Shah also extended modern education, particularly technical education, and founded a modern hospital system. During his reign, attempts at industrialization were made in an effort to relieve Iran's reliance on imports. The system of tax collection was improved and the increased revenue was used to reconstruct parts of Tehran and to build roads and railways, such as the Trans-Iranian railway.

16 The Shah of Iran with the Empress Farah. Rapid westernization during his autocratic rule alienated large sections of the country's predominantly Muslim population.

THE REIGN OF MUHAMMAD REZA SHAH

During his reign Muhammad Reza Shah failed to use newly acquired wealth from oil revenues to improve the conditions of the mass of the people. His grandiose plans of modernization based on western methods, and known as the "White Revolution", only served to create more inequality and an increased feeling of frustration among much of the population.

By 1977 severe social and economic problems resulted from his ambitious programmes. Agricultural production had not increased despite the Shah's much publicized land reform launched in 1963 as the central feature of the "White Revolution". This meant that much of the country's food had to be imported, and

24

about half the rural population went hungry. Inequalities in income and standard-of-living existed within the urban areas themselves, and between the capital city, Tehran, and the provinces. Fabulous wealth contrasted with extreme poverty.

There was growing realization that oil revenues would decline after the mid-1980s. Despite heavy state subsidies in an attempt to diversify industry, productivity remained poor and Iranian goods could not compete in the international market. By 1978 western commercial banks had lent Iran about US $ 5,000 million with commitments for a further US $ 3,000 million. The Shah had pursued a policy of spending a huge amount on the military to protect the throne and to sustain his desire to make Iran the dominant regional superpower. The cost of this was a rate of oil production which was impossible to maintain and a dependence on imports which accelerated inflation. State officials were often corrupt and incapable of implementing reform.

A diplomat, in a report to his government about Iran, wrote: "The problem of the Shah is that he wants to drive his people to the garden of Eden with a stick". It was an accurate comment on the Shah's regime.

THE RE-EMERGENCE OF OPPOSITION TO THE SHAH

Immediately after the 1953 coup the Shah, with the help of the armed forces and the newly established secret police, the notorious SAVAK was able to dismantle all opposition to his regime. Amnesty International reported in 1976

The suppression of political opposition is carried out by SAVAK with extreme ruthlessness using a system of informers which permeates all levels of Iranian society and which has created an atmosphere of fear remarked on by visitors to Iran and emphasized by opponents of the regime outside the country.

However, in 1977, there emerged a new and vocal opposition of a kind not seen since the early 1960s. It was made up of several very different groupings. There were secular reformers, led by the National Front, who

7   The Shah of Iran visiting a new petrochemical plant at Bandar Shahpur, one of the ruler's ambitious schemes to transform Iran into a major industrialized country.

demanded a modern constitution, the abolition of the monarchy and the introduction of some socialist measures. They found much of their support among the professional and salaried middle classes. Then there were the secular radicals, who were divided into the Fedayi, a militant Marxist guerrilla organization, the Tudeh or Communist Party, the Revolutionary Tudeh and the Marxist-Leninist Organization. The Marxist left, as a whole, has little mass following in Iran and support is limited to university students, white collar associations and some trade unions. Finally, there was the religious opposition to the Shah, itself divided into conservatives, radicals and reactionaries. More than any other opposition grouping, the religious ones mobilized a mass following, especially among the bazaar population (shopkeepers, merchants and craftsmen), the shanty-town poor, and even the industrial workers.

This can be explained by a number of factors. First, while the regime crushed all grass-root organizations belonging to the secular opposition, it permitted the bazaar guilds, the clergy, the seminaries and the local mosques to function. In fact, the oil-boom of the early 1970s brought prosperity to the seminaries and thereby increased the ranks of the lower clergy. By 1977 the religious institutions were the only organizations in the country left free of state domination. Not surprisingly, public opposition to the Shah became concentrated in the mosques. Second, during the 1970s a religious revivalist movement swept the country, affecting especially the lower middle classes and the shanty-town poor. Like Methodism in nineteenth-century England, Islam and more particularly the Shi'a branch dominant in Iran, provided the urban poor with a much-needed sense of community. In such a situation it was easy for one man, whether a John Wesley or an Ayatollah Khomeini, to appear as the saviour of the common people. Finally, the Marxist left was hurt during the 1970s by the fact that both the Soviet Union and China openly supported the Shah.

The various opposition groups increasingly gathered around one man, the 78-year-old religious leader, the Ayatollah Khomeini. He became the symbol of opposition to the Shah. The Ayatollah Khomeini had been at the forefront of opposition to the Shah before, in the early 1960s when the armed forces struck at peaceful demonstrators, killing thousands in Tehran alone. The government had then exiled the Ayatollah, who took refuge in Najaf, the Shi'a holy city in neighbouring Iraq. Later, when the Iraqis expelled him, he went to Neauphle-Le-Château, a Paris suburb. In exile, he continued to denounce the Shah and resolutely refused to compromise. This unswerving integrity of purpose and fearless opposition to tyranny propelled him to become undisputed leader of the opposition movement to oust the Shah.

By the end of 1977 opposition to the Shah had become widespread. There were mass protest assemblies in the universities and in 1978 dozens of Iranian towns were shaken by demonstrations and riots. These began in regional centres, the holy city of Qom and Tabriz, and then spread in May to over thirty cities and towns including the capital Tehran, where the bazaar area was occupied by troops and closed down on several occasions. Hundreds died in these events.

It was not so surprising that the Shah, with so much opposition, decided to allow some changes in the political system. The total ban on press reporting was loosened, albeit slightly, and the Shah announced free elections for a Majlis to be convened in June 1979. However, this was all a case of too little too late. There were further demonstrations in Tehran, which led the Shah to declare martial law on 19 August. A devastating fire occurred in a cinema in the oil town of Abadan. It killed 400 people. The opposition was left in no doubt as to who was responsible for this action — SAVAK.

The government of Prime Minister Jamshid Amuzegar had lost control of the situation and it was replaced by a new administration headed by Jaafar Sharif Emami, himself the grandson of a religious leader. The new government took several measures to calm the opposition — casinos were closed and censorship on films increased. These failed to pacify the opposition movement, and in early November the Shah dismissed Sharif Emami and appointed a military government under the leadership of General Ghdam Reza Azhari.

Demonstrations still continued. On 4 September (the end of the Holy month of Ramadan) demonstrators in Tehran demanded the restoration of the constitution and the creation of a republic. And some, more ominously, chanted "Death to the Shah". Further marches were banned, but on 7 September 300,000 people took to the streets. The Shah responded by declaring martial law again in Tehran and in eleven other cities. Opposition reached a high point on 8 September when troops clashed with demonstrators and

3000 people were killed in the Jaleh Square in Tehran, a tragedy which became known as "Bloody Friday". The political situation continued to deteriorate rapidly. Strikes in the southern oilfields cost Iran an estimated US$ 30 million a day. Industries were forced to close down for lack of raw materials. Many foreign companies suspended operations in the face of mounting hostility and violence against foreigners. Americans were singled out in particular because of US support for the Shah. Ordinary people were opposed to the introduction of western ideas and moral codes such as the emancipation of women. Attacks on banks and cinemas reflected popular anger at the Shah's policy of enforced westernization.

THE LAST DAYS OF THE SHAH

Opposition to the Shah's regime intensified. The whole country was seething with violence and chaos. Rumours began to circulate that the Shah was about to leave the country, although these were strongly denied by supporters of the monarchy. However, on 16 January 1979 the Shah, by all accounts dispirited and only a shadow of his former self, departed for what was officially described as a holiday. Few believed that he would return. Before his departure the Shah appointed Shapur Bakhtiar as Prime Minister and head of a Regency Council. Bakhtiar was an opposition leader who had supported the nationalist Musaddiq in the 1950s. He was seen by many as merely the Shah's puppet, and so his government had little chance of surviving the storm which raged around it. Of vital importance was the attitude of the armed forces. Some observers feared a military coup followed by the kind of repression witnessed in Chile after the overthrow of Allende. Others feared a civil war.

With the departure of the Shah, the armed forces lost their cohesion. The Shah's military commanders had never enjoyed personal loyalty among the rank and file and his departure broke the lines of command. There were daily reports of mutinies and desertions. A parade of thousands of troops through the streets of Tehran on 31 January 1979, intended as a show of government force, only served to highlight the armed forces' divided loyalties. Several troop carriers displayed pictures of Khomeini. To wild

18   Vast crowds of supporters surround the motorcade of the Ayatollah Khomeini on his return to Iran from exile on 1 February 1979. In the background is the huge Shayad or Shah Memorial near the airport in Tehran, one of the city's major landmarks.

cheering from the crowds, some soldiers kissed the pictures and others shouted that they were "with the people".

THE AYATOLLAH KHOMEINI RETURNS

In desperation Prime Minister Bakhtiar attempted to negotiate with Khomeini, but the Ayatollah refused and condemned the government as illegal, calling on his supporters to continue the battle. After some delay Khomeini himself arrived in Tehran on 1 February to an emotional welcome from several million people. A brave but futile rearguard action mounted by Bakhtiar came to an end when the armed forces deserted him. For two days Iran teetered on the brink of civil war as Khomeini's supporters attacked army bases. Then the army backed away, troops were ordered back to barracks and the senior officers declared the army's neutrality. Bakhtiar resigned as Prime Minister and went into hiding.

The Shah's regime had been successfully toppled by the revolutionary movement. The Ayatollah Khomeini and the mixed religious, moderate and leftist forces he led were victorious. Iran was proclaimed an Islamic Republic. Mehdi Bazargan, a veteran politician, long active in opposition politics, was installed as the new Prime Minister. But real power

remained with the Ayatollah, who became the *de facto* head of state, and his Revolutionary Islamic Council. The new regime ruthlessly sought out those officials who had served during the Shah's reign, and Islamic Revolutionary Courts were set up to try them. Over 300 were executed by firing squad during the first six months of the new regime, including former commanders of the armed forces, members of the hated secret police, ministers in the Shah's government and a former Prime Minister, Amir Abbas Hoveyda. The exiled Shah was con-

19   February 1979. The Ayatollah Khomeini, after his return from exile, announces that he will form an Islamic Revolutionary Council to seize power from the civilian Prime Minister, Shapur Bakhtiar.

20 February 1979. Followers of the Ayatollah Khomeini drag a statue of the Shah to the Ayatollah's headquarters.

demned to death *in absentia*.

During 1979 severe punishments were introduced in order to enforce strict Islamic codes of behaviour. Alcohol was banned and women were required to dress modestly. Even mixed bathing, kung fu films and karate were banned. These measures and the continued paralysis of the economy, mounting unemployment, and rising inflation alienated increasing numbers of Iranians. At the same time unrest erupted among Iran's numerous ethnic minorities. The Kurds in the northwest and the Arabs in the oil-rich province of Khuzistan clashed with forces trying to maintain the authority of the central government.

Despite the claims of religious leaders, including the Ayatollah Khomeini, a considerable number of Iranians came to dispute that the revolution was fundamentally religious. The popular mandate given to Khomeini ran out when the Shah was ousted from power. Ideally, leftists, moderates and others who supported the revolution would have liked to see Khomeini withdraw to the holy city of Qom and leave politics and administration to them.

YOUNG HISTORIAN

A

1 Outline the main problems facing Iran at the beginning of the twentieth century.
2 Give some examples of Reza Shah's policy of modernization.
3 Write a short biography of (a) Reza Shah; (b) Ayatollah Khomeini.
4 Write a paragraph on each of the following: (a) the Majlis; (b) the Cossack Brigade; (c) SAVAK.
5 There were several different opposition groups responsible for the 1979 Revolution but the religious groups were the most successful — why?
6 Describe the main problems facing the government of the Ayatollah Khomeini.

B

1 You are a foreign affairs reporter for a British newspaper. Write a short article tracing the growth of the opposition movement in Iran in 1978.

2 Imagine you are a young supporter of the Ayatollah Khomeini, writing a letter to your parents in which you describe the scenes at Tehran airport when the Ayatollah returned in February 1979.

C

1 Write the newspaper headlines which might have appeared above reports on: (a) the Civil War in Iran (1909); (b) Reza Khan proclaimed Shah in 1926; (c) the return of Muhammad Reza Shah in 1953; (d) "Bloody Friday", September 1978; (e) the departure of the Shah from Iran in January 1979.

D

1 Draw a map showing the spheres of influence of Britain and Russia in Iran in 1907.
2 Draw a map showing the partition of Iran in 1948.

THE ARAB WORLD AFTER THE FIRST WORLD WAR

The Turkish retreat from the Arab Lands at the end of the First World War led to the partition of the Ottoman Empire, and almost the whole of the Middle East came under European control. The victorious Allies convened a peace conference in Paris in 1919 to decide what should be done with the territories they had wrested from the Ottoman Empire. The inhabitants of these areas were not represented at the conference, even though both Arab and Jewish battalions had participated in the war effort on the side of the Allies. Delegations were sent by various religious and national groups, however, to press their claims. The Great Powers haggled and bargained between themselves, and Great Britain endeavoured to reconcile the conflicting promises she had made at various stages in the war to the Arabs, the French, and the Zionists, in order to win their support in the struggle. In these promises, and in the dispositions made at the Peace Conference lie the seeds of conflict that have since riven the Middle East.

By the end of the First World War public opinion in the west had turned against the old aggressive colonialist policies. Instead, people favoured the principles of "self-determination" and "consent of the governed" as expressed by President Woodrow Wilson of the United States. This reinforced the hopes of independence cherished by the peoples of the Ottoman Empire. However, the British and French Governments were still intent on preserving and strengthening their overseas empires. To the British this meant controlling the route to India, i.e. the Suez Canal, Palestine, Iraq, which contained the Mosul oil-fields, and the Persian-Arab Gulf. The French were concerned to continue their historical role of carrying civilization and culture to Syria, Lebanon and the Holy Land.

The solution found was to institute the Mandate: the newly liberated peoples would gradually be educated for self-government under the tutelage of a western power, who would withdraw when the country was ready for independence — a judgement left wholly to the mandatory power. The Mandate system was imposed on most of the Arab territories at a new peace conference at San Remo in 1920, and severely disappointed them.

THE HUSAIN — McMAHON CORRESPONDENCE 1915-1916

In the course of 1915 the Sharif Husain of Mecca, who entertained hopes of becoming king of a large Arab state, had exchanged a series of letters with McMahon, the British High Commissioner in Cairo. In them he had obtained promises of British support for a vaguely defined Arab state in the Fertile Crescent and Arabian Peninsula in return for his leading an Arab uprising against the Turks. The boundaries of the state were not precisely defined at the time and became the subject of bitter recriminations, as Britain endeavoured to reconcile this commitment with later promises made to others. In June 1916 Husain proclaimed the Arab Revolt against the Turks in which his son Faisal and T.E.Lawrence played a leading part.

THE SYKES — PICOT AGREEMENT 1916

This crudely imperialist treaty arose out of a

29

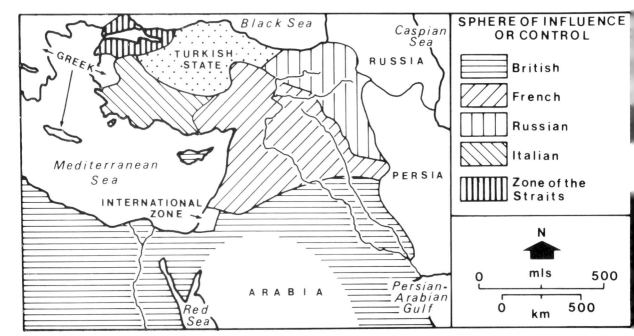

The map legend reads:

SPHERE OF INFLUENCE OR CONTROL

- British
- French
- Russian
- Italian
- Zone of the Straits

21   The Sykes-Picot Treaty of 1916, showing plans for the partition of the Ottoman Empire.

series of negotiations between Georges Picot and Sir Mark Sykes, on behalf of the French and British Governments. It arranged to divide the Ottoman Empire into French and British spheres of interest and influence which would be mutually respected. It also recognized Russian claims to certain territories in the Middle East. The secret agreement was made public by the Bolsheviks after the Russian Revolution of 1917. The settlement which resulted from the Paris and San Remo peace conferences conformed closely with the interests defined in it.

THE BALFOUR DECLARATION 1917

In 1917 the British issued the Balfour Declaration, stating that the British government favoured the establishment of a Jewish National Home in Palestine. The Zionist movement had been growing in strength since its beginning in the late nineteenth century among the persecuted and suffering Jewish communities in Eastern Europe.

The First Zionist Congress in Basle, in 1897, had been led by Theodor Herzl, who is recognized as the founder of political Zionism. It

stated that "Zionism strives to create for the Jewish People a home in Palestine secured by Public Law". When Zionist appeals to the Sultan of Turkey for permission to immigrate and settle there had failed, Herzl realized that the support of one of the Great Powers was essential for success. Germany espoused the Zionist cause for many years, but failed to persuade the Sultan to yield. The Balfour Declaration of 1917 was therefore hailed as a major achievement.

Jewish and Arab relations later deteriorated into active hostilities, but in 1919 the leading spokesmen on both sides expressed a readiness to cooperate. Whether out of genuine goodwill or good diplomacy, Faisal, the principal spokesman of Arab interests, and Dr Weizmann, the Zionist leader, agreed to negotiate every dispute beginning with boundaries, in a spirit of concord

THE DIVISION OF TERRITORIES

In the final settlement which emerged from the Paris and San Remo peace conferences, the lands of the Ottoman Empire were carved up between the Great Powers, and only a small independent Arab State emerged. This was the Kingdom of the Hejaz in the Arabian Peninsula. Sharif Husain was recognized as its ruler.

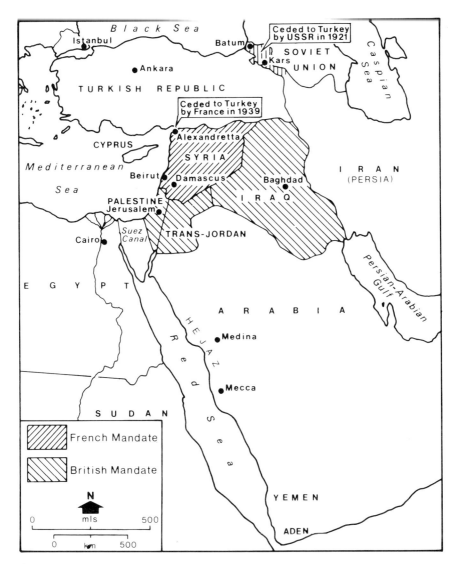

A number of new states were created, and a glance at the map will show how unnaturally straight many of the boundaries are. France was given a Mandate over Syria (redefined as a much smaller area), Cilicia and the Lebanon. Britain was awarded a Mandate over Palestine, Iraq, and a new "desert-state" between the two, named Transjordan. She retained her protectorate over Egypt, while Italy extended her control over Libya.

The new states thus created lacked homogeneity and any sense of national identity. In the Ottoman Empire loyalty was traditionally directed to the Sultan as head of Islam, or to one's own national or religious millet. It was not defined by geography but by cultural identity. Syria, Lebanon, Palestine and Iraq all contained considerable communities of Armenians, Kurds, Druzes, Circassians, Shi'a (heterodox Muslims), Greek and Syrian

22   The Middle East after the Treaty of Lausanne, 1923.

Christians, Jews and other minority groups, with their own languages and customs, who felt themselves no part of an Arab Muslim state and feared domination by the Sunni majority. The instability and frictions caused by the presence of these large minorities still plague these countries, in spite of a growing sense of national identity over the years.

THE FALL OF SHARIF HUSAIN AND THE RISE OF IBN SA'UD

Sharif Husain did not long enjoy his kingdom of the Hejaz. Having lost British support by opposing the Balfour Declaration, he alienated his remaining supporters in Islam by proclaiming himself Caliph in 1924 — a claim not generally recognized. His old rival in the Arabian Peninsula, Abdul Aziz Ibn Sa'ud, had revived the ideals of the strict *Wahhabi* movement in Islam in 1910, and built up a powerful centralized organization. He had steadily extended his power and swallowed up other provinces, and he seized the opportunity to move against Husain in 1924, declaring him a traitor to Islam. By 1926 he had conquered the Hejaz and was recognized as king of the territories later known as Saudi Arabia.

THE BEGINNINGS OF ARAB NATIONALISM

The earliest Arab nationalist writings had appeared in the second half of the nineteenth century, principally in Syria and Egypt. These countries were the most exposed to western European power, culture and educational influence. Conscious of Ottoman weakness and backwardness, people were concerned to reinvigorate Islam and the Islamic state. In defending Islam, they needed to stress Arabic studies and this led to the first stirrings of Arab pride in their heritage and the beginnings of an Arab nationalist sentiment. A few Arab Christians in Syria also became interested in the Arab revival and they adopted as their own the Islamic heritage with which their language was so closely linked. These ideas were confined to a few individuals, mostly western-trained, and in the early days they were concerned with revivifying the Ottoman Empire by rousing a sense of Ottoman nationality.

Arabism began to spread and gain strength after 1908, when Arab hopes for some degree of autonomy were disappointed and resentment grew at the increasingly forceful attempts by the Young Turks to impose Turkish officials and the Turkish language on Arab provinces. However, the overwhelming majority of Arabs remained loyal to the Ottoman Empire and to the Sultan as the head of the Islamic State.

23   The Arab Revolt. The Emir Abdullah accepts the surrender of a Turkish commander, 1917.

THE ARAB REVOLT AND THE ARAB KINGDOM

Ambitious to win an independent kingdom, Sharif Husain, the Hashemite ruler of Mecca, had initiated negotiations for British support in 1915 and as a result he agreed to head an Arab revolt against the Turks. Two secret nationalist groups in Syria made contact with him at the beginning of 1915 in the hope of rising against Ottoman rule and founding an independent Arab kingdom comprising Syria, Palestine, Iraq and the Arabian Peninsula. A large number of nationalists were hanged in Damascus in 1915 and 1916 by Djemal Pasha, the Turkish military governor, for treason and became the first nationalist martyrs.

Sharif Husain proclaimed the Arab revolt in the Hejaz in June 1916 and its success proved a great stimulus to Arab nationalist feeling. Faisal, Husain's third son, who led the Arab troops into Damascus with Allenby and established an autonomous government there under the military administration, had become its leading spokesman. He headed a delegation to the Paris peace conference to press the Arabs' claim for independence. In March 1920 he proclaimed the independent kingdom of Greater Syria (which included Palestine and Iraq). This did not suit the Great Powers, however, and in April 1920 France was awarded Mandates over Syria and the Lebanon, and Britain Mandates over Palestine and Iraq. In July 1920 French troops occupied Damascus and the Arab Government was deposed.

In reaction to this virtual annexation of much of the Middle East by Britain and France, there was a sharp increase in Arab nationalist feeling during the inter-war years and the Arabs intensified their demand for freedom from foreign control. In some countries the nationalists resorted to armed rebellion.

FRENCH TROUBLES IN SYRIA

The French, anxious to protect their colonial interests and pursue their civilizing mission, were aware that only among the Maronite Christians of Mount Lebanon could they expect much support. They created an enlarged State of Lebanon, taking in the Muslim coastal strip

24 General Allenby leaving the Jaffa Gate after the British military occupation of Jerusalem in January 1918.

of Beirut and Tripoli, and divided the rest of Syria into four small administrative units. The Sanjak of Alexandretta, with its large Turkish element, was ceded to Turkey in 1939, to the lasting bitterness of the Syrians. The reason the French gave for carving up the country was that they needed to protect the large minority groups. But this policy of divide-and-rule was resented as such, and smouldering rebellion exploded in the great Druze Revolt of 1925-1926 which quickly spread to the cities. French reaction was severe and Damascus was bombarded twice in the course of re-conquest.

After this eruption, however, constitutional plans were drawn up and negotiations for some degree of independence dragged on until the Second World War. The imposition of a Mandate and the failure to introduce full representative institutions fostered extreme nationalist feelings, which were not at all

33

appeased by the educational, administrative and cultural efforts expended by the French during the Mandate period.

25 Sa'ad Zaghlul, the Egyptian nationalist leader who pressed for Egyptian independence from British rule.

BRITISH TROUBLES IN EGYPT

The Egyptian government had been dominated by the British Agent and Consul-General from 1883-1914 after Egypt had been brought to the verge of bankruptcy by the Khedive Ismail.

British control gradually tightened and increasing numbers of British officials ran the administration. After Turkey declared war on the Allies in 1914, Britain assumed a Protectorate over Egypt to ensure defence of the Suez Canal. The first High Commissioner to be appointed under this new regime was Sir Henry McMahon.

Egyptian nationalist feeling had been growing since the end of the nineteenth century, prompted by such men as Lutfi al-Sayyid, Aziz Ali al-Misri and exiles from Syria. Martial law, censorship and the hardships suffered by the Egyptian people as a result of British military involvement in the First World War all combined to intensify opposition to the British Protectorate. The nationalist movement, which was anti-British and anti-Fuad (the British-nominated Sultan, later king of Egypt), capitalized on this discontent.

In 1918, at the end of the war, a delegation (in Arabic Wafd) led by Sa'ad Zaghlul demanded autonomy, but the British government refused to treat with the nationalists and Zaghlul and the other leaders were deported. This action sparked off riots and demonstrations in 1919 and, in an attempt to conciliate public opinion, the British freed the deportees. The members of the Wafd and their supporters continued to press for total independence and Britain again attempted first to crush and then to appease them. The Wafd was supported by all sections of the Egyptian people: Muslims, Copts, students, pashas and peasants, and on one occasion the women of Cairo marched through the streets in their all-enveloping black cloaks to demonstrate for independence.

In 1922 Britain proclaimed the end of the Protectorate and the "independence" of Egypt. But she reserved to herself the right to dictate on four matters: the security of imperial communications in Egypt, defence, foreign affairs, and the Sudan, which was ruled in condominium (joint control) with Egypt. This was a first step, but it by no means satisfied the Wafd, which had transformed itself into a political party. It did not recognize the British Proclamation because of its compromised nature. The success so far achieved by the Egyptian nationalists was due largely to the courage and steadfastness of Zaghlul and to the solidarity shown by the Egyptian people. Britain was unable to find a political group willing to cooperate with her in order to defeat the emerging nationalist movement.

In 1923 a constitution and parliamentary system on the European model was instituted, and for the next thirty years Egyptian politics were the scene of a three-cornered struggle for power between Britain, the Egyptian Crown and the political parties.

BRITAIN'S MANDATED TERRITORIES

The British Mandated territory of Transjordan was largely a patch of desert between Palestine and Iraq. It was ruled throughout the inter-war period by the Sharif Husain's second son, Abdullah, as an emirate, and after 1946, as a kingdom. It was essentially a period of tranquillity and consolidation, ruled by the king's immediate circle, with support from the British. Transjordan experienced none of the troubled nationalist agitation of its neighbours.

Circumstances were quite different in neighbouring Iraq, with its developed nationalist aspirations and large non-Arab minorities of Kurds and Assyrians. The modern state of Iraq was created in 1921, and the British offered its throne to Faisal, who had fled from Syria as the French were occupying it. Faisal was the ablest of the Hashemites, and his intelligence and active goodwill enabled Iraq to gain a large degree of independence relatively early. By a series of treaties culminating in that of 1930, Iraq was declared an independent nation but bound firmly to Great Britain in matters of foreign policy and military facilities.

The British Mandate in Palestine was fraught with difficulties, largely of Britain's own creating and was the scene of intense Arab nationalist demonstrations.

During the inter-war years the dream of a United Arab State faded. Each part of the Arab world turned its attention to its own special problems and interests created by the arbitrary division of the Fertile Crescent and Mesopotamia into a number of new states.

THE PALESTINE PROBLEM AND THE EMERGENCE OF ISRAEL

Britain's Mandate for Palestine was confirmed by the Council of the League of Nations on 29 September 1923 when the Mandate came formally into operation. From the outset the British administration was faced with the impossible task of trying to reconcile two opposing nationalisms — one Jewish, under the name Zionism, the other Arab. Since 1917 the British government had been committed to support the establishment of a Jewish National Home in Palestine. On 2 November 1917, even before the British army had occupied Palestine, the British Foreign Secretary, Arthur Balfour, had issued his famous Declaration in the form of a letter to Lord Rothschild of the Zionist Federation:

His Majesty's Government view with favour the establishment in Palestine of a national home for the Jewish people, and will use their best endeavours to facilitate the achievement of this object, it being clearly understood that nothing shall be done which may prejudice the existing civil and religious rights of existing non-Jewish communities in Palestine, or the rights and political status of Jews in other countries.

The terms under which the Mandate for Palestine was granted to Britain reaffirmed the Balfour Declaration. They provided that "an appropriate Jewish agency" should be established which would advise and cooperate with the Palestine Administration in matters affecting the Jewish national home and take part in the development of the country. In effect, the Jewish Agency for Palestine, set up by the Zionist Organization, quickly became a state within a state, determined to transform Palestine into nothing less than an exclusively Jewish state. It encouraged large-scale Jewish immigration into a territory which at the beginning of the Mandate was overwhelmingly Arab in population. The Jewish population of Palestine rose from a mere 8 per cent of the total in 1918 to roughly one third by the end of the Second World War. Between 1918 and 1948 almost a quarter of a million acres of land were purchased by Jews, mainly from Syrian and Lebanese absentee landlords living outside Palestine. The Arab tenants were evicted from these lands to make room for Jewish agricultural colonization. Only Jewish labour was employed on Jewish farms and in Jewish factories, and the employment of Arab workers was strictly prohibited. In this way a distinct and separate Jewish economy, organized on rigidly national lines, was created in Palestine.

The Arab majority, Muslim and Christian, bitterly opposed the Balfour Declaration and Jewish immigration, and called for the prohibition of land sales to Jews. Like other Arabs in the Middle East, the Palestinian Arabs had been led to believe that they would gain independence after the First World War, and they would settle for nothing else. Britain, however, would not give in to their demands to abolish the Mandate, nor would she concede unlimited immigration to the Zionists. When appeals, protests, arguments, demonstrations and local riots failed to move the British administration, the Arabs resorted to violence. Violent demonstrations of Arab feeling occurred in 1920, 1921 and 1929. They were followed in 1936 by a general strike, called by the Mufti of Jerusalem and the Higher Arab Committee. This paralysed the economic life of the country for about six months, and was accompanied by an outbreak of guerrilla activity in the hills around Nablus.

The appointment of a British Royal Commission on Palestine and the intervention of neighbouring Arab rulers brought this phase to an end in October 1936. But rebellion broke out again in September 1937 after the Commission had recommended partitioning the country. A full-scale British military effort was needed to bring resistance to an end. In 1939, having abandoned the partition plan, the British Government published a White Paper proposing that 75,000 more Jews should be admitted over five years and then Jewish immigration would cease. In addition, the Arabs were to be protected against land purchase and land acquisition by the Zionist Agency. Finally it proposed that self-governing institutions should be set up at the end of the five years. This would have preserved the Arab majority in the country and its legislature.

THE NAZI HOLOCAUST

By the time the White Paper appeared, the horrifying Nazi policy of exterminating Jews in Europe had already begun and was to reach even more frightening proportions after the outbreak of the Second World War. Zionists and Jews generally regarded the White Paper as a betrayal of the terms of the Mandate. When David Ben Gurion, Chairman of the Jewish Agency Executive, was in New York in 1942, an Extraordinary Zionist Conference held at the Biltmore Hotel utterly rejected the White Paper and made a new statement of Zionist policy. The declaration of the conference issued on 11 May 1942 concluded:

> The conference urges that the gates of Palestine be opened; that the Jewish Agency be vested with control of immigration into Palestine and with the necessary authority for upbuilding the country, including the development of its unoccupied and uncultivated lands; and that Palestine be established as a Jewish Commonwealth integrated into the new structure of the democratic world.

This policy put the Jews on a collision course with the British authorities in Palestine. Many of the Jews in Europe who escaped the Nazi holocaust tried to reach Palestine with organized

Zionist help, but the British authorities, in accordance with the 1939 policy, took strong measures to prevent illegal immigration. Wretched vessels crowded with refugees were turned away and, in view of Jewish misery in Nazi-occupied Europe, such tragic actions merely served to intensify the bitter propaganda campaign against British policy in Palestine that was being waged in the United States and elsewhere. In the end the British authorities failed to stem the rising tide of Jewish immigration. The new immigrants greatly strengthened the illegal military organizations which had been formed by the Jewish Agency — the Haganah and its units of shock troops, the Palmach, together with two smaller extremist groups the Irgun Zvaei Leumi, led by Menachem Begin, and the Stern Gang. Towards the end

of the war, with the aim of imposing the Biltmore programme, they embarked on a policy of violence against British personnel and installations. Among their most dramatic acts of terrorism was to blow up the King David Hotel in Jerusalem on 22 July 1946. The Government Secretariat and part of the military headquarters were housed in the hotel. About 100 Government officials, British, Arab and Jewish were killed.

Exhausted after the war with Germany, Britain was no longer in a position to impose a solution on Palestine. On 18 February 1947 the British Foreign Secretary, Mr Bevin, announced in the House of Commons that the British Government had found that "the Mandate has proved to be unworkable in practice, that the obligations undertaken to the two communities have been shown to be irreconcilable". In desperation, on 2 April 1947 Britain referred its Mandate over Palestine back to the League of Nations' successor, the United Nations.

26 A crowd of 20,000 at Madison Square Park, New York protest against British policy in Palestine after the Jewish refugee ship *Exodus* was rammed by a British warship off Haifa in July 1947.

27 The destruction of the King David Hotel in Jerusalem by Zionist forces on 22 July 1946.

THE PALESTINE PROBLEM BEFORE THE UNITED NATIONS

The United Nations General Assembly sent a Special Commission to Palestine to investigate the situation. Its report, issued on 31 August 1947, proposed two plans: a majority plan for the partition of Palestine into two States, one Jewish and one Arab, with economic union; and a minority plan for a federal State. The Assembly adopted the majority plan on 29 November by 33 votes for, to 13 against, with ten abstentions. The plan divided Palestine into six principal parts, three of which (56 per cent of the total area) were reserved for a "Jewish State" and the other three, with the enclave of Jaffa, (43 per cent) for an "Arab State". Jerusalem was to be

an international zone administered by the UN as the holy city for Jews, Muslims and Christians.

The Arabs, who formed a clear two-thirds majority of the population, rejected the Partition Plan on the grounds that it violated the United Nations Charter by denying them the right to decide their own destiny. They also pointed out that in the proposed Jewish State 50 per cent of the population were Arab, while Jews owned less than ten per cent of the total land area. After the voting on the Partition Resolution, disorders broke out in the country — the Arabs calling for a three-day strike and demonstrations as a sign of protest; the Jews celebrating their political victory. In the subsequent disorders some 1700 people on both sides were killed.

Alarmed by the violence, the UN hesitated and began to reconsider its proposals for partition. The Jewish Agency, fearful that victory would be snatched away from them at the eleventh hour, opposed any delay in establishing

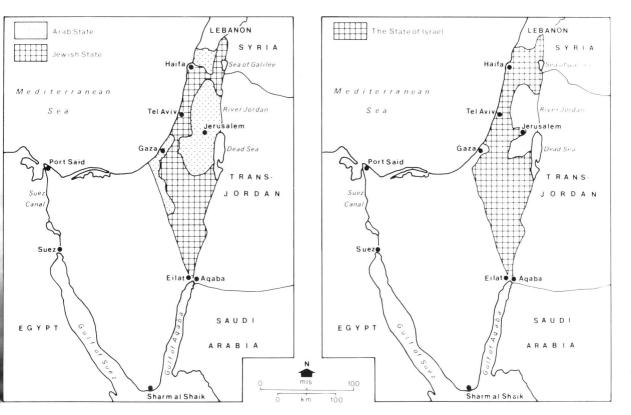

28   The UN plan for the partition of Palestine.

29   The State of Israel after the 1948 war.

the Jewish State and took the law into their own hands. The Haganah and its two splinter groups, the Irgun Zvaei Leumi and the Stern Gang, launched attacks against the Arab inhabitants within the territory assigned to the Jewish State under the Partition Plan, and also outside it. In the words of the Zionist leader David Ben Gurion: "As April [1948] began our War of Independence swung decisively from defense to attack". One such attack was the tragic massacre of 250 men, women and children in the Arab village of Deir Yasin on 9 April 1948 — an incident which accelerated the panic flight of Palestinian Arabs. During the six-month period before the Mandate was terminated and the British left, some 400,000 Palestinian Arabs were driven from their homes to become refugees.

THE BIRTH OF THE STATE OF ISRAEL

On 14 May 1948 British troops in Palestine were withdrawn to the port of Haifa as a preliminary to the final evacuation of the territory. The British Mandate finally came to an end. Immediately, the Jewish authorities in Palestine officially proclaimed the State of Israel, and at once the new state was recognized by the United States and a little later by the Soviet Union. A provisional government was formed in Tel Aviv the day before the Mandate ended, with David Ben Gurion as Prime Minister and other members of the Jewish Agency Executive in leading ministerial posts. The constitution and even the electoral laws of the new state had already been prepared.

In response to the declaration of the State of Israel, the Secretary-General of the newly formed League of Arab States informed the UN that the Arab states "were compelled to intervene for the sole purpose of restoring peace and security and of establishing law and order in Palestine". The armies of the neighbouring Arab states crossed the frontiers into Palestine.

In the conflict which followed, an Egyptian force crossed the Sinai desert and advanced north through mainly Arab territory towards Tel Aviv, halting before the first Israeli defence line. Jordan's Arab Legion, which had been ordered

39

30 Two members of the Haganah, the illegal military organization established by the Jewish Agency in Palestine, being arrested by British troops in Jaffa during 1947.

to occupy the central highlands, was diverted by an Israeli attempt to seize the Old City of Jerusalem. On 9 June 1948 the UN ordered a four-week truce. During this time Israel received much-needed reinforcements of aircraft, heavy and small arms and volunteers from abroad. The arms came mainly from Czechoslovakia and were paid for by funds raised by Israel's supporters, mainly in the United States. On 10 June 1948 Israeli Premier Ben Gurion declared:

Our bounds are set wider, our forces multiply, and we are administering public services, and daily new multitudes arrive.... All that we have taken we shall hold. During the cease-fire, we shall organize administration with fiercer energy, strengthen our footing in town and country, speed up colonization and *Aliyah* (immigration) and look to the army.

When the truce ended, a well-organized Israeli army with a small but effective airforce and navy was ready to give battle in what was for them a desperate struggle for the survival of the new state.

In contrast, the Arab effort was seriously impaired by lack of unity and coordination, and there was constant friction between Egypt and Transjordan. Israel proved more than a match for them. When the second phase of the Arab-Israeli war came to an end in July 1948 only the mountainous districts of central

Palestine plus a narrow strip around Gaza remained in Arab hands and even Jerusalem was threatened by a finger of Israeli territory reaching up from the Plain of Sharon to the city's Jewish suburbs on the west. A series of armistice agreements were concluded at Rhodes during 1949 between Israel and her Arab neighbours, Egypt, Lebanon, Transjordan and Syria. They left Israel in control of over two thirds of Palestine instead of the 56 per cent allotted to the Jewish State under the UN Partition Plan. These agreements did not establish peace, only an unsteady truce between Israel and her neighbours.

The rump of Palestine, left in Arab hands, consisted of two separate parts — the hill country now known as the West Bank, held by the Transjordan army, and the Gaza strip held by the Egyptian army. In Gaza the Egyptians set up the so-called "All Palestine Government", under the Mufti of Jerusalem, while King Abdullah of Transjordan held a Palestinian conference at Jericho which accepted his rule. Transjordan then became the Hashemite Kingdom of Jordan. Despite the UN resolution to internationalize it,

Jerusalem remained divided between Israel and Jordan. Israel transferred the parliament and government from Tel Aviv to west or Jewish Jerusalem and made it the capital city, though it remains unrecognized by the UN.

By the time the last armistice agreement had been signed, a further 350,000 Palestinian Arabs had been forced to leave the country, bringing the total number of refugees expelled from their homes inside Israel to some 750,000. On 11 December 1948 the UN General Assembly resolved that:

> the refugees wishing to return to their homes and live at peace with their neighbours should be permitted to do so at the earliest possible date, and . . . compensation should be paid for the property of those choosing not to return and for loss of or damage to property which, under principles of international law or in equity, should be made good by the Governments of authorities responsible.

Though the UN annually reaffirmed the right of the refugees to repatriation or compensation, Israel refused to implement the resolution and instead demanded the resettlement of the refugees in Arab countries.

31   David Ben-Gurion proclaiming the birth of the State of Israel in Jerusalem, 14 May 1948.

The Zionist dream of a State of Israel had been achieved but only by the total disruption and displacement of those "non-Jewish communities" whose rights had been guaranteed in the Balfour Declaration and the Mandate.

32 Some of the Palestinian Arabs who were driven from their homes to become refugees after the creation of the State of Israel in 1948.

YOUNG HISTORIAN

A

1 Write a short paragraph on either (a) the Husain—McMahon Correspondence, 1915—1916; or (b) the Sykes—Picot Agreement, 1916; or (c) the Balfour Declaration, 1917.

2 Explain in three short paragraphs the following: (a) the Mandate System, (b) Zionism, (c) the Wahhabi Movement.

3 Why did the European partition of the Ottoman Empire fail?

4 Trace the beginnings of the Arab nationalist movement.

5 Write a short account of either (a) the British Protectorate in Egypt, 1914—1922 or (b) the British Mandated territories.

6 Why was the Jewish Agency Executive opposed to the British Mandate?

7 Why did the Arabs oppose the main proposals of the UN Special Commission Report on Palestine?

B

1 You are a member of the Arab nationalist movement. Write a letter to your parents in which you explain why you have joined it.

2 Imagine that you are a war correspondent for a newspaper. Prepare a short report on the first Arab/Israeli struggle in 1948.

C

1 Write the newspaper headlines which might have appeared above reports on: (a) the declaration of the Kingdom of Greater Syria, 1920; (b) the Druzes Revolt, 1925—26; (c) the British Government's White Paper on Jewish immigration; (d) the creation of the State of Israel in May 1948; (e) the armistice agreements between Israel and her Arab neighbours in 1949.

THE RISE AND FALL OF NASSERISM

The post-war years were a time of political unrest and revolution in the Arab Middle East. Following the Second World War demands to end foreign political influence dominated national politics. Although the French Mandate over Syria had terminated in 1941, French influence continued until 1946 when French troops were finally forced to leave the country. In Egypt and Iraq attempts to revise the treaties which had been made with Britain failed. A second force which had a decisive influence on the national politics of the Arab states was the creation of the State of Israel and the subsequent defeat of the Arab armies in the 1948 Arab-Israeli War. The defeat was a bitter humiliation for the Arab armies and undermined the authority of the ruling groups in Syria, Egypt and Iraq. The increasing political unrest in the region resulted in the Egyptian revolution of 1952, the 1958 revolution in Iraq and a series of military *coups d'état* in Syria.

THE EGYPTIAN REVOLUTION

The defeat of the Arab armies in 1948 had greater repercussions in Egypt than in the other Arab countries, since the government in Cairo had considered itself the leader of the Arab struggle. As a result of the defeat, the popularity of the King, Farouk, a dissolute and pleasure-loving monarch, declined dramatically and continual changes of government took place. The instability caused by the Palestine situation and the uncertainty over relations with Britain created a state of political confusion. British intervention in Egyptian internal

33   King Farouk of Egypt who was deposed by Nasser and the Free Officers in 1952.

affairs during the Second World War had led to a sharp rise in anti-British feeling. In the post-war period two issues, which originated from the terms of the 1936 Anglo-Egyptian treaty, were the main points of disagreement between the Egyptians and the British. The Egyptians demanded the withdrawal of British troops stationed in the Canal Zone, and the union of Egypt and the Sudan. In 1951 the Wafd government, in a last bid for royal and popular support, revoked the 1936 Anglo-Egyptian treaty. Egypt claimed sovereignty over the Sudan and attacks were made on British bases in the Canal Zone. Following a British counter-attack on the auxiliary police headquarters in Ismâiliya, later known as "Black Saturday", auxiliary police in Cairo mutinied and terrorists set fire to British and foreign-owned buildings in Cairo. The Wafd government was forced to resign and the time was ripe for revolution.

The revolution of 20 July 1952 was carried out by a group of army officers who called themselves the Free Officers. This group, which had been set up as early as 1939, was led by Colonel Gamal Abdul Nasser. The army head-quarters were occupied and the revolutionaries soon gained control over key communications and services. Within four days Egypt was entirely in the hands of the revolutionaries and King Farouk was forced to abdicate. At first Nasser remained in the background and General Neguib, an associate of the Free Officers, was elected President of the Revolutionary Command Council.

The new regime concerned itself with three main issues. Firstly, in September 1952 land reform measures were introduced whereby land-holdings were limited to 200 *feddans* in area (one feddan = approximately one acre). This measure was designed to break the political power of the large landowners who had dominated political life under the monarchy. Secondly, the government turned to the Sud-anese problem. General Neguib had been chosen as the figure-head of the new regime partly on account of his Sudanese origins, in the hope that this might encourage Sudan to unite with Egypt. In February 1954 an Anglo-Egyptian agreement was reached on Sudan. The Egyptians accepted Sudanese independence, hoping and expecting that Sudan would later unite with Egypt. But these hopes were disappointed. Thirdly, the Revolutionary Command Council was eager to secure the withdrawal of British troops from the Canal Zone. In October 1954 an Anglo-Egyptian agreement on Suez was signed, by which British troops would withdraw within twenty months.

In June 1953 the monarchy was abolished and Egypt was declared a republic. Neguib became both President and Prime Minister. A struggle for power developed between Neguib and Nasser who was Deputy Prime Minister. By November 1954 Nasser had succeeded in gaining power from Neguib and had become President of Egypt.

44

POLITICAL UNREST IN SYRIA

The defeat of the Syrian troops in the 1948 war with Israel weakened the ruling conservative group in Syria led by Shukri al-Quwatli. The humiliation felt by the military increased army interference in internal political affairs.

In 1949 a military *coup d'état* was led by Colonel Husni al-Zaim. There followed a period of political instability during which a rapid succession of military leaders took charge of Syrian affairs. Between 1949 and 1951 Colonel Adib Shishakli emerged as a strong political leader and by 1951 a military dictatorship headed by him was established. In 1953 a new constitution was drawn up and Colonel Shishakli was made President. Yet another coup took place in 1954 and the first Syrian President, Shukri al—Quwatli, was installed again as head of state in 1955.

During the next two years the international and internal position of Syria deteriorated. Anti-western feeling, still running high after the struggle for independence, was strengthened by opposition to the newly created Baghdad Pact and the events of the Suez crisis. Political life came to be dominated by the left-wing Arab Baath party. The Baath had been founded in 1949 by Michel Aflaq, a Greek Orthodox Christian born in Damascus. Disenchanted with both the nationalists and the communists, he preached a vague and abstract blend of nation-alism, socialism and democracy, which proved to have a strong appeal to the young and ideal-istic, especially among the army officers. Until 1958 the Baath cooperated with the communists, but as the Syrian Communist Party began to strengthen its position it threatened the authority of the Baathists. In order to avoid a communist take-over, the Baath Party sought to rescue the situation by uniting with Egypt, thus strengthening the nationalist position. Syria and Egypt joined to form the short-lived United Arab Republic in 1958.

REVOLUTION IN IRAQ

In Iraq, too, the Arab defeat in the 1948 war contributed to the political instability of the post-war period. The humiliation felt by Iraqi troops undermined the army's support for the conservative and pro-western regime of strongman Nuri Said. After 1954 this regime was further weakened by Nuri Said's dictatorial methods, which included the dissolution of parliament and a ban on all political parties.

During the 1950s the international policies adopted by Iraq diverged more and more from those of other Arab states. Nuri Said underestimated the importance of Arab nationalism and the strength of anti-British feeling. He continued to pursue a political course which stressed relations with the west rather than Arab solidarity, and in 1955 Iraq formed a military alliance, the Baghdad Pact, with Iran, Pakistan, Turkey and Britain. The Suez Crisis of 1956 further increased anti-western feeling in Iraq and throughout this period riots and demonstrations expressed public dissatisfaction with the government.

34   General Nuri Said, the Prime Minister of Iraq (on right) seen here with the Iranian Prime Minister during a meeting of the Baghdad Pact in Tehran in 1956.

The climate of opinion in the rest of the Arab world was characterized by nationalist and anti-western feelings associated with the rise of Nasserism and the establishment of the United Arab Republic. The pro-western standpoint of the Iraqi regime was heavily criticized by nationalist groups within the country. Shortly after the union of Egypt and Syria in 1958, Iraq and Jordan responded by forming the Arab Federation, but the union did not survive the revolution.

On 14 July 1958 an army coup carried out by units stationed near Baghdad heralded the Iraqi revolution. The young king, Faisal II, together with his uncle, the Crown Prince, and Nuri Said were brutally murdered. Two days after the coup the masses, whom Nuri had tried to help through his programmes of development, exulted at his death and dragged his corpse through the streets of Baghdad. The new regime was headed by Brigadier Abd al-Karim Kassem who became Prime Minister of the newly proclaimed republic. At first it seemed that the Arab nationalists would gain power and that

Iraq would join the United Arab Republic, but within a few months it became clear that Kassem had chosen to follow a course of independent nationalism and, as a result, the Deputy Prime Minister, who was pro-Nasserist, was dismissed. The communist party on the other hand gained favour for a time with Kassem. Iraq withdrew from the Baghdad Pact in 1959, a gesture which dramatically illustrated the end of the country's close alliance with the west.

NASSER AND THE SEARCH FOR ARAB UNITY

The charismatic personality of Gamal Abdul Nasser dominated the history of both Egypt and the Arab Middle East during his presidency from 1954 to 1970. During the first few years following the 1952 revolution in Egypt the basic ideas and policies which were to direct the course of Nasser's regime were established. Encouraged by the success of the revolution, Nasser became committed to the cause of Arab nationalism and Arab unity under Egyptian

35   The Egyptian President, Gamal Abdul Nasser, at Dhahran, Saudi Arabia in September 1956 during talks with King Saud of Saudi Arabia (centre) and Syrian President Shukri al-Quwatli (left) on the Suez Crisis. The cordiality of the meeting proved to be shortlived and later Nasser's influence within the Arab Middle East aroused suspicion and hostility among the more conservative Arab States.

leadership. In his attempt to secure freedom from foreign political dominance he pursued a policy of non-alignment with either of the major power blocs. He viewed Arab solidarity and unity as the key to the political freedom of the Arab Middle East. The revolution had given Egypt the opportunity to gain wider influence. Indeed, Nasser soon became the hero of Arab unity and leader of the Arab world.

A number of events confirmed Nasser's political standpoint. In 1955 Nasser attended the Bandung Conference which was a meeting of the world's non-aligned states. His anti-western feelings were expressed when he acted as a leader of Arab opposition to the Baghdad Pact. The Baghdad Pact was a military alliance between Iraq, Iran, Pakistan, Turkey and Britain and to Nasser it symbolized the persistence of western interference and influence in the Arab countries. Egypt began to express openly anti-western feelings and to make its political position of non-alignment clear. An arms agreement was concluded between Egypt and Czechoslovakia, and in 1956 Egypt officially recognized the Communist regime in China.

THE SUEZ CRISIS, 1956

Egyptian opposition to the Baghdad Pact caused relations with the west to deteriorate rapidly. Britain, the USA and the World Bank withdrew their offers of financial support for the construction of the Aswan High Dam as a result. Nasser, however, was determined to continue with the project, if necessary without western aid, for he regarded it as vital for Egypt's development. He immediately announced that the Suez Canal Company, which was owned mainly by French and British interests, had been nationalized. Revenues from canal dues would be used to pay for the new dam.

French and British protests and a stepping-up of the vicious propaganda war against Nasser had no effect. In retaliation, Britain and France came to a secret agreement with Israel to make a coordinated attack on Egypt. On 29 October 1956 Israeli troops invaded Sinai and the Gaza strip. Britain and France called for a ceasefire between Israel and Egypt and for the installation of a Franco-British peace-keeping force at Port Said. Egypt refused to accept this proposal. On 31 October Anglo-French air operations against Egypt began, and troops were landed at Port Said. American and Soviet opposition to the attacks led to a ceasefire supervised by the United Nations Emergency Force. The Anglo-French and the Israeli troops then withdrew, and the canal, which had been blocked by the Egyptians during the crisis, was reopened in 1957.

Instead of destroying Nasser, Suez transformed him into a world figure, a leader of international stature. It was a great political victory. He was never again to be concerned solely with Egyptian affairs. He had become the undisputed leader of the Arabs. Talking about the Suez affair after it was all over Nasser reflected:

If Eden [then British Prime Minister] had come with the British Navy and tried to

36 Headlines of the national British newspapers for 31 October 1956 when British and French troops invaded Egypt.

invade Egypt I think the Egyptians would have forgiven and forgotten once it was all finished. Even if he had come with the French we would have said that perhaps he needed an ally. But to bring the Israelis into an adventure against the Arabs was very foolish. We were used to hating British policy but then we began to despise British policy. I hate to use the word despise, but it is the only one.

EGYPT AND SYRIA

The union of Egypt and Syria in 1958 to form the United Arab Republic extended Nasser's influence within the Arab Middle East. There were high hopes for the success of the union which represented an important achievement in Nasser's drive for Arab unity. In a rousing speech in Damascus in 1961 Nasser launched a vigorous attack on critics of the union:

We tell them that the Union is stronger and will grow stronger. We are determined about the Arab Unity and we follow the road of Arab Unity. Imperialism tries to tell the Arabs everywhere that this Union has not succeeded ....They try to convince the other Arab

47

countries and nations that the experience of unity between Egypt and Syria is faltering in its footsteps and that the people of Syria are tired of this experience. Why? They try to do this in order that they may destroy the idea of Arab Nationalism and the idea of Arab Unity.

When Nuri Said, Nasser's main rival for leadership of the Arab world, was swept from power by the Iraqi revolution in 1958, it seemed as if Egyptian dominance of the Fertile Crescent was about to be realized. However, the Nasserists did not gain power in Baghdad, and the new Iraqi regime, with support from the communists, followed an independent line, hostile to Egypt. Other Arab states declined Nasser's invitation to join the union, and only the new republican

37 In spite of the efforts made by President Nasser the search for Arab unity has proved elusive.

regime in Yemen, supported by Egyptian arms established a rather loose association with the United Arab Republic.

The union with Syria itself proved to be short lived. Under Nasser's presidency of the United Arab Republic, Egypt soon came to dominate the partnership. In Syria the Egyptian-inspired socialist policies were resented, especially by the influential merchant class. Nasserism was regarded with growing suspicion also by the more conservative Arab states. Encouraged by their support, the Syrian army staged a takeover in 1961 which ended the union. The collapse of the union was a damaging blow to Nasser's vision of Arab unity.

ГИДРАВЛИЧЕСКИЙ СХЕМА

Further attempts at union were made. In 1963, following changes in the regimes of both Syria and Iraq, an agreement was reached to establish a federation of Egypt, Syria and Iraq. Rivalries between the two main political groups — the Baath party and the Nasserists — still existed in Iraq and Syria. For this reason, Egypt decided to withdraw from the federation later that year. The issue of union arose again in 1965, but Nasser had little enthusiasm for the idea.

EGYPT AND THE SOVIET UNION

Following the Suez Crisis of 1956 Egypt turned for assistance to the USSR, which had been watching Nasser's progress with a mixture of hostility and fascination. The Anglo-French-Israeli attack on Suez brought Nasser and Krushchev, who was to become the Prime Minister of the Soviet Union in 1958, much closer together. Russia's support of Egypt's position, both in the United Nations and outside,

38 After the Suez Crisis the USSR began to supply arms and military equipment to rebuild the Egyptian forces. Here Egyptian army recruits are introduced to the secrets of modern tank warfare.

played a vital part in mobilizing world opinion against the aggression. The USSR agreed to finance the Aswan High Dam and to supply arms and military equipment to rebuild the Egyptian forces. Although he was ready to accept aid from the USSR, Nasser remained determined to maintain his political position of non-alignment. He was strongly opposed to communism and his regime persecuted and imprisoned Egyptian communists. During a visit to Moscow in 1958 Nasser informed Krushchev:

We are not going to allow the Communist Party in the United Arab Republic. We do not think those Communist Parties understand or correctly analyse the nature of the national movement in under-developed countries, and we are not going to allow them. I am not ready to listen to anything about those Communist Parties.

49

On another occasion he declared:

> We shall not hand the nation over to imperialism and the reactionaries, nor shall we hand it over to communism and dependence, but we will remain patriotic, nationalist, solely for the sons of the Arab nation.

This sort of anti-communist propaganda displeased the Soviet leaders and there were many heated arguments between Krushchev and Nasser. Egyptian insistence on Arab nationalism became an embarrassment to the Kremlin and relations between the two countries were often strained.

In 1961 Egypt introduced a number of socialist policies — banks, industries, large stores, main hotels and trading organizations were nationalized. These measures contributed to the breakdown of the union with Syria, but found favour with the Soviet leaders. During the 1960s the domestic situation continued to deteriorate. Egyptian debts to the USSR had increased, there were conflicts within the government, and acts of terrorism multiplied. When the United States stopped giving Egypt food aid in 1965, the USSR, determined to hold on to its political influence in the Middle East, came to occupy an even more influential position in Egyptian political and economic affairs.

EGYPT AND THE PALESTINIANS

After the collapse of the union with Syria Egypt turned to other political issues in the Middle East. For example, from 1962 to 1967 Egyptian forces fought a long and costly war in support of the new republican regime in Yemen, which was engaged in a bitter struggle against royalist forces still loyal to the deposed ruler, the Imam. The failure of the United Arab Republic had threatened Nasser's role as a leader of the struggle for Arab unity. Eager to regain this position, Nasser took up the Palestinian cause by supporting and encouraging the setting up of the Palestine Liberation Organization (PLO). Nasser's initial enthusiasm for the PLO was shortlived and by 1966 Syria, not Egypt, was its chief supporter. In 1967 Nasser was criticized by his Arab neighbours for his lack of action on the Israeli situation and for not helping Syria during border clashes between Syria and Israel.

Nasser reacted to this criticism by closing the Straits of Tiran at the entrance of the Gulf of Aqaba to Israeli shipping. Israel regarded this as a declaration of war and on 5 June 1967 the Six Day War broke out. Egypt's forces were rapidly defeated by Israel and put to flight. An estimated ten thousand Egyptian soldiers were killed or died of thirst in the desert. At the end of the war Israel had made substantial territorial gains, including the whole of Sinai and the Gaza strip taken from Egypt. As a result of the war the Suez Canal was closed. Littered with wrecks, it became a battle line between two hostile neighbours. Fierce fighting along the canal and Israeli air strikes deep into Egyptian territory continued from 1968 to 1970 despite attempts by the United Nations to prevent it. During this "War of Attrition" the Egyptian cities in the Canal Zone were almost entirely destroyed.

Nasser resigned following the 1967 defeat, but his resignation was not accepted. A popular outpouring of support in massive demonstrations, only partly stage-managed, called on Nasser to stay in office. He agreed to remain as President but described his mood after the defeat as like "a man walking in a desert surrounded by moving sands not knowing whether, if he moved, he would be swallowed up by the sands or he would find the right path". Although Egypt reaffirmed its confidence in Nasser, he had lost much of his status in the Arab world. His relations with the conservative Arab states had been hostile (in 1958 King Sa'ud of Saudi Arabia had paid nearly two million pounds to have a bomb put on Nasser's plane) but he was now forced to turn to them for financial help after Egypt's defeat. At the Khartoum Conference in 1970 Saudi Arabia and Kuwait together with Libya, agreed to compensate Egypt for the revenue lost due to the closure of the canal.

Egypt rebuilt its forces after the Six Day War mainly with Soviet assistance. Russian supplies were limited, however, and many of the promises of arms were never fulfilled. Nasser's relations with the USSR reached a turning point in 1970. The USSR refused to send Egypt the arms it had asked for and this left Nasser with little choice but to accept the Rogers Plan proposed by the United States. The Rogers Plan provided for a 90-day ceasefire to the escalating violence of the War of Attrition between Egypt and Israel, during which time negotiations for a peaceful settlement would take place, under the supervision of the United Nations. Nasser's acceptance of the plan in 1970 was strongly criticized by the PLO.

Nasser's last political act was to negotiate a ceasefire between the Palestinian leader Yasser Arafat and King Husain of Jordan, whose forces had been locked in a savage civil war in Jordan in 1970 known as "Black September". The ceasefire, agreed at a summit of Arab heads of state in Cairo, was the final service Nasser rendered to the Arab people, and the sustained work and worry cost him dear. Already exhausted and ill, he died of a heart attack on 28 September 1970 at the age of 52. At the news of his death the whole of Egypt became engulfed in a wave of emotion. People travelled from all over the country and from many parts of the Arab world to Cairo until there were over ten million in the city. At Nasser's funeral the vast crowds became wild with grief. Five divisions of troops were moved in to control the mourners, but the crowds were so enormous that the soldiers were swept away and the funeral procession mobbed and almost wrecked. The Egyptian people cried "The lion is dead, the lion is dead". Mohamed Heikal, Nasser's great friend and political adviser, later wrote:

> The Lion was dead but his achievements have lived on. He tied Egypt to the rest of the Arab world and he tied the Arabs to the contemporary world and its ideas. He did not realise the total Arab Unity that he dreamed of and worked for, but he crystallized the need for it. During his time this unity proved impossible to achieve. But after him, it has become impossible to ignore.

EGYPT UNDER SADAT

The charismatic Nasser was succeeded as President of Egypt by Anwar el-Sadat, an unprepossessing character and an unknown quantity in Egypt. Few believed that Sadat was a man of sufficient stature ever to play Nasser's role.

Sadat's early political career had been directed by his vision of an independent Egypt. During the 1940s he was a leading member of the revolutionary movement which had been developing in the armed forces. He was one of the Free Officers, and Nasser made him a member of the Revolutionary Command Council after the 1952 revolution. Sadat held various senior positions under Nasser but never enjoyed any real power. When he became President most people were uncertain as to his ability and his political leanings, whether to the left or to the right wing. A popular story of the time conveys these impressions: when the chauffeur of the presidential car reached an important intersection he asked Sadat for direction.

> "But which way did Nasser usually go?" asked Sadat. "At such times he usually went left, your excellency". "Ah", replied Sadat. "Well, signal that we're going left and then turn sharply to the right".

The new President seemed slightly stunned to find himself in such an exalted office. "You have invested me", Sadat confided to his people, "with an honour which God knows, has never crossed my mind throughout my life; nor have I striven for it". Gradually, however, the self-effacing Sadat began to show unsuspected qualities of shrewdness and toughness, and he embarked on new initiatives of his own.

Under Sadat, Egypt was to follow a very different course from that taken under Nasser. Nasser had shunned the west and maintained close political relations with the Soviet Union, leaving the country politically isolated. When Sadat became President, Egypt faced severe economic and political problems. The country was still suffering from the effects of the disgrace of the 1967 military defeat. Sadat viewed peace with Israel as an essential step in improving Egypt's economic and political position. For this reason, from 1970 onwards, he was firmly committed to finding a solution to the Egyptian-Israeli conflict.

Both the economic and political policies followed by Sadat reflected his opinion that the United States must play a key role in resolving the conflict with Israel. Although a Soviet-Egyptian Treaty of Friendship was signed in 1971, the influence which the Soviet Union had enjoyed in Egypt during the 1960s was never re-established. Sadat's acceptance of the Rogers Plan marked his desire for renewed political relations with the United States.

Sadat declared 1971 a "year of decision". On 4 February he announced a new "initiative". In exchange for a limited, rather than total, Israeli withdrawal to the Sinai passes, he promised to re-open the Suez Canal, extend the ceasefire and begin peace talks. The Israelis did not accept this suggestion and constantly delayed peace talks with Egypt. Sadat's much-heralded "year of decision" ended with no significant progress towards peace.

Meanwhile Sadat had become disillusioned with the Soviet Union. The arms supplies promised by Soviet leaders were never delivered. Sadat was also not prepared to accept continued Soviet interference in Egyptian affairs. In 1972 Soviet military advisers in Egypt, estimated to number some six thousand, were expelled. This action emphasized Sadat's anti-Soviet feelings and was intended to improve Egypt's relations with the United States in the hope of enlisting their support towards progress on peace negotiations.

THE 1973 OCTOBER WAR

While Israel benefitted from the standstill in peace negotiations, Egypt faced economic collapse and domestic problems of worker unrest. Military expenditure totalled almost one third of the national income. Egypt was also heavily in debt to the Soviet Union due to the purchase of Soviet arms supplies. Between 1967 and 1973 the situation of "no war — no peace" became increasingly frustrating for Egypt. In 1971 Sadat had tried to replace the military struggle by peace talks. His failure to make any progress forced him to return to the battlefield.

On 6 October 1973 Egypt attacked Israeli bases in Sinai. Within two days two armies, hundreds of tanks and a forward air-defence screen of SAM-6 surface-to-air missiles had crossed the Suez Canal, plunging deep into the Egyptian territory that Israel had occupied since 1967. This invasion took Israel completely by surprise and the Israeli forces suffered heavy losses of equipment and men in the early stages of the war. But, when it seemed that their

39   Israeli forces advance into Egypt after crossing the Suez Canal during the 1973 October War. After their initial setback, the Israeli forces quickly demonstrated their military superiority, advancing to within 45 miles of Cairo, the Egyptian capital.

military defences had been broken and the road from Sinai to Tel Aviv lay open to the Egyptian forces, Israel rallied and quickly began to demonstrate her military superiority. After some delay the United States began a massive airlift of vital military supplies to Israel. On 19 October Sadat accepted a ceasefire, realizing that further United States intervention on behalf of Israel would be disastrous for Egypt.

Although Egypt did not "win" the October War in any conventional sense, it represented a political and psychological triumph for Sadat who soon earned the title of "Hero of the Crossing" from the jubilant Egyptian people. He had set out to destroy the Israeli Security Theory of occupying land as a means of defending the State of Israel. He had succeeded in penetrating the Israeli defence system. The victory strengthened his national and international position in the conflict, giving Egypt a stronger negotiating position.

THE DISENGAGEMENT AGREEMENTS

Henry Kissinger, the American Secretary of State, acted as a mediator during negotiations after the October War, to establish a disengagement agreement. The first disengagement agreement was signed on 18 January 1974. During 1974 and 1975 Kissinger continued negotiations with both sides, in his famous "shuttle" diplomacy, and after a long period of talks the second disengagement agreement was agreed in September 1975. As a result of this agreement Israel withdrew from the Mitla and Giddi Passes in Sinai and Egypt got back the valuable Abu Rudais oil-field. This agreement also marked the end of fighting between the two countries — "the conflict shall not be resolved by military force but by peaceful means". On 5 June 1975 President Sadat took the bold step of reopening the Suez Canal to international shipping.

SADAT'S PEACE INITIATIVE

Following the disengagement agreements of 1974 and 1975, the attempts which were made to continue peace talks faced delays and continual disagreements over arrangements. On the economic front, Sadat adopted what has been termed an "Open Door" policy. By this he hoped to attract foreign investment to the private sector of Egypt's mainly state-controlled economy, particularly from the United States and the oil-rich Gulf States such as Kuwait and Saudi Arabia. Response to the Open Door policy was disappointing and the economic situation worsened. The Soviet Union's refusal to let Egypt delay the repayment of debts only aggravated the crisis in the Egyptian economy.

In January 1977 Sadat's government decided to remove the price subsidies on such basic commodities as rice, sugar and cooking-gas, in response to pressure from the International Monetary Fund. Massive demonstrations, the most destructive since the 1952 revolution, then erupted in Egypt's major cities. At the height of the demonstrations some 30,000 protestors battled with the police in Cairo alone. There were cries of "Down with Sadat" and "Nasser, Nasser, Nasser". Favourite targets were symbols of the new wealth in Egypt, such as the large American and German cars, that were stoned and burned, while several night clubs along the "golden strip" leading to the pyramids were ransacked. Before order was restored, an estimated 79 had been killed, 1000 wounded and 1250 jailed. The official explanation blamed left-wing agitators and "communist elements" for the rioting. In reality, the disturbances originated from the social strains created by Sadat's Open Door policy. Many people felt that Sadat's strategy for economic recovery had produced several hundred new millionaires at the expense of millions of poor Egyptians.

The poor economic situation increased the pressure on Egypt to make peace with Israel. The cost of arms was crippling the economy, and foreign investment was not forthcoming while the conflict with Israel remained unresolved. Sadat, extremely frustrated by the slow progress, was forced to take a further initiative. In November 1977 Sadat made a historic trip to Jerusalem. In a dramatic speech before the Israeli Parliament, the Knesset, on 20 November 1977 he declared his desire for peace:

> In all sincerity I tell you we welcome you among us with full security and safety. This is itself a tremendous turning point....We accept to live with you in permanent peace based on justice.

53

40   19 January 1977 — a trolley bus burns in a Cairo
street set on fire by rioters protesting against increased
food prices.

Sadat's trip to Jerusalem was a surprise to other
Arab leaders, and his public recognition of the
State of Israel made them furious. In his speech
Sadat identified the need to solve the problem
of the Palestinian people as central to any plan
for peace. He claimed to be seeking peace for
the whole area, not just peace between Egypt
and Israel.

THE ROAD TO PEACE

Although Sadat's peace initiative was welcomed
by both the Egyptian and Israeli people, a
number of Arab states — Libya, Algeria, Iraq,
Syria and the People's Democratic Republic of
Yemen — set up a "Rejection Front" to oppose
him. Summit talks between Egypt and Israel
were held on Christmas Day, 1977 at Ismâilîya.
It was clear that the two sides were still a long
way from reaching a peaceful solution. During
later meetings US President Jimmy Carter and

Sadat remained divided on the issue of Palestinian
self-rule. President Carter was anxious to secure
a separate peace agreement between Egypt and
Israel, and intervened personally to prevent the
talks from collapsing. Following the announce-
ment of the Framework for Peace, agreed at the
Camp David talks between Carter, Sadat and the
Israeli Premier Begin in September 1978, it
became clear that an Egyptian-Israeli peace
agreement would not be conditional on an
agreement for Palestinian self-rule. Instead, it
would involve only a limited commitment to
further negotiations on the future of the
Palestinian people. Sadat had been forced to
compromise and make a series of concessions
before Israeli intransigence and strong American
pressure.

On 26 March 1979 the Egyptian-Israeli Peace
Treaty was signed. The Treaty claimed to be an
important step towards peace within the whole
area. The state of war between Egypt and Israel
would be ended and Israel would withdraw its
armed forces from Sinai, returning it to
Egyptian control. The withdrawal would begin
from the north coast. Within nine months Israel
would have moved east of a line from El Arish
to Ras Muhammad. After three years the
boundary of the former Mandate of Palestine

41 American television broadcast these scenes from the Israeli Parliament in Jerusalem during President Sadat of Egypt's historic speech there on 20 November 1977.

would become the international boundary between Egypt and Israel. Friendly relations between the two countries would begin after the first stages of the withdrawal. Trade and economic barriers would be lifted and ambassadors exchanged. For its part, the United States promised to provide substantial financial backing to both countries.

The rest of the Arab world, radical and conservative states alike, denounced the treaty and Sadat for signing it. Egypt, they said, had not honoured the Arab policy that there could be no peace agreement unless, first, Palestinian self-rule had been established. PLO leader Yasser Arafat called the treaty "a crime against the Arab nation" and attacked Sadat personally

42 At the Camp David talks on Middle East peace in September 1978 President Sadat of Egypt was forced to compromise and to make a series of concessions before the intransigence of Israeli Prime Minister Begin.

for "betraying Egypt, the Arab nation, and the Palestinian cause by selling Jerusalem for a handful of sand in Sinai". Meeting in Baghdad, the Arab states agreed to boycott Egypt by cutting off diplomatic and financial aid. The Arab League headquarters were withdrawn from Cairo and this represented a particularly damaging blow to Egypt's prestige. However, despite Egypt's new isolation in the Arab world, Sadat maintained that the peace treaty with Israel was a very important achievement for Egypt and that in the last analysis his complex international acrobatics were aimed at improving the life of ordinary Egyptians. The majority of the good-natured Egyptian people probably believed him. Yet the rest of the Arab world felt that there could be no lasting peace within the region as long as the rights of the Palestinian people were ignored.

YOUNG HISTORIAN

A

1 Discuss the results of the defeat of the Arab armies in 1948 in Egypt, Syria and Iraq.

2 Discuss the factors leading up to either: (a) the revolution in Egypt, 1952 or (b) the revolution in Iraq, 1958.

3 What were the main problems facing the new revolutionary government in Egypt?

4 Write short accounts of the following: (a) the Baghdad Pact; (b) the Israeli invasion of Sinai, 1956; (c) the "Open Door" policy of President Sadat.

5 What were the implications of the "Suez Crisis" for President Nasser?

6 Discuss attempts to unite Syria with Egypt — why did they fail?

7 Why was Russia interested in improving relations with Egypt in the early 1960s and why did this relationship deteriorate in the late '60s and early 1970s?

8 Assess how successful recent American peace initiatives on the Middle East have been.

B

1 Imagine you are a newspaper reporter. Write a short article reporting the funeral of President Nasser.

C

1 Write the newspaper headlines which might have appeared above reports on: (a) the revolution in Egypt 1952; (b) the nationalization of the Suez Canal in 1956; (c) the death of Nuri Said in 1958; (d) the closure of the Straits of Tiran in 1967; (e) the food riots in Cairo in January 1977; (f) President Sadat's visit to Jerusalem in November 1977.

ISRAEL AND ITS NEIGHBOURS AFTER 1967

In the mid 1960s in Israel there was a notable increase in Palestinian guerrilla activities from across the frontiers of Egypt, Jordan and Syria. Israel blamed the Arab states from which the raiders came, and retaliated with heavy punitive attacks against Jordan and Syria.

THE JUNE WAR 1967

By April 1966 the situation between Syria and Israel had become explosive after artillery and aerial fights, and Israel deployed large military forces on the border. President Nasser of Egypt warned Israel against attacking Syria, dismissed the UN forces stationed on the Israeli-Egyptian border since 1956, and closed the Gulf of Aqaba to Israeli shipping. In June 1967 Jordan joined the fight and the third Arab-Israeli war broke out, lasting six days.

Israel won a sweeping victory, capturing the Gaza strip and the whole of Sinai up to the Suez Canal. From Jordan, Israel took the West Bank, including Arab Jerusalem, and from Syria the Golan Heights. The conquest of Old Jerusalem gave Israel access to the Western Wall, the only standing remains of the Temple of the Lord founded by Solomon and the most sacred place of worship for all Jews. They had been denied access to it since 1948. Israel immediately tore down the barriers, reunited East and West Jerusalem and applied Israeli law to the whole, despite the UN resolution which called upon it to stop changing the status of the holy city revered by the Jews, Muslims and Christians alike. Israel made it plain from the beginning that there could be no question of returning Old Jerusalem to Arab possession in any peace settlement. Another wave of refugees fled from the West Bank to Jordan, but nearly a million Arabs remained under Israeli occupation.

At first, Israel's decisive victory over the

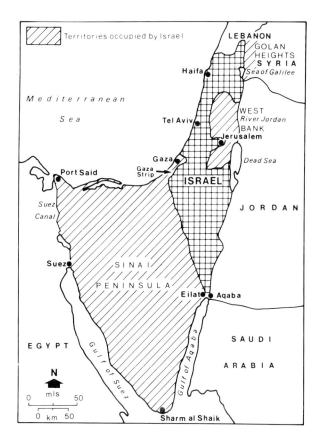

43   Territories occupied by Israel during the Six Day War 1967.

Arab states raised hopes that a settlement to the nineteen-year-old Arab-Israeli conflict might be possible. As soon as a ceasefire had brought an end to the fighting, the United Nations and the world powers busied themselves with the search for peace. On 22 November, after many attempts, the UN Security Council agreed to Resolution 242 put forward by the British delegate, Lord Caradon. The Resolution was to remain the basis of all subsequent peace initiatives during the next five years. It emphasized that the establishment of a just and lasting peace in the Middle East should include the application of the following principles: (i) withdrawal of Israeli armed forces from territories occupied in the recent conflict; and (ii) termination of all claims or states of belligerency and respect for and acknowledgement of the sovereign, territorial integrity, and political independence of every State in the area, and their right to live in peace within secure and recognized boundaries free from threats or acts of force. The Council affirmed also the necessity for (a) guaranteeing freedom of navigation through international waterways in the area, and (b) achieving a just settlement of the refugee problem.

The now famous Resolution precariously bridged the gap between the Arab and Israeli positions but, before efforts to implement it could get under way, the attitude of both sides in the dispute hardened. Although the Israeli Prime Minister had declared on the eve of the war that Israel had no intention of annexing "even one foot of Arab territory", the Israeli Knesset or Parliament had since legislated the so-called "reunification" of Jerusalem, and Israeli forces had destroyed a number of Arab villages. These actions, together with the establishment of Jewish settlements in the occupied territories, appeared to confirm Arab fears of Israeli expansionist designs.

As hopes of peace faded, the trend towards violence accelerated. Palestinian guerrilla raids led to heavy Israeli reprisals, particularly against Lebanon, and Egypt and Israel began a destructive artillery duel across the Suez Canal. In order to undermine the Egyptian regime, the Israelis initiated a series of deep penetration bombing raids on targets inside Egypt. American efforts brought about a ceasefire between Israel and Egypt in 1970, but progress towards even a partial peace settlement foundered on Israel's insistence that it would in no circumstances withdraw to the pre-June 1967 lines.

THE "YOM KIPPUR WAR"

In the autumn of 1973 the Arab-Israeli conflict appeared to be further than ever from solution. The Israelis were confident that their military superiority over the Arabs had increased. They remained in control of all the territories occupied in 1967, where they had established some 50 military and paramilitary settlements. However, their confidence was to be shattered when Egyptian and Syrian forces launched an attack on two fronts on 6 October 1973. The Israelis were taken completely by surprise. 6 October was Yom Kippur, the Day of Atonement, the most important religious festival in Israel, when all public services were suspended. This made it difficult for the Israelis to mobilize their forces rapidly to meet the emergency.

Egyptian forces crossed the Suez Canal, broke through the heavily fortified Bar Lev line and moved up to the Mitla Passes in Sinai. The Syrians, in a coordinated move, broke through the Israeli line in the Golan Heights and were stopped only a few kilometres from the Jordan River. Israeli casualties were high, and the use of sophisticated Soviet ground-to-air missiles and anti-tank missiles in some of the biggest tank battles in history, took a heavy toll in men and equipment.

Despite the Arab forces' initial advantage, the Israelis made a remarkable recovery. Israeli forces managed to cross the Suez Canal and encircle the Egyptian Third Army. On the Syrian front, Israel recaptured the Golan Heights and advanced within 35 kilometres of the Syrian capital, Damascus. An uneasy ceasefire came into effect on 25 October. The fighting had continued for three weeks.

The situation between Israel and its neighbours remained volatile, and there were sporadic incidents along both the Egyptian and Syrian fronts. It was only after intensive "shuttle" diplomacy by the US Secretary of State Henry Kissinger that Israeli-Egyptian negotiations were held in November 1973, and a disengagement agreement was not concluded until January 1974. The Israelis withdrew to a line about 30 kilometres from the Canal; the Egyptians agreed to reduce their army on the east bank of the Canal and to repopulate the area. A buffer zone occupied by UN forces separated the two sides. A disengagement agreement with Syria proved more difficult and was only concluded in May

44   The Israeli-occupied Golan Heights; an Israeli self-propelled cannon fires at Syrian positions during one of the artillery exchanges here which continued until a disengagement agreement was concluded between Israel and Syria in May 1974 following the Yom Kippur War.

1974 after yet another round of Kissinger's "shuttle" diplomacy. The Israelis withdrew roughly to the lines of before the 1973 war and prisoners of war were exchanged.

The Yom Kippur War deeply disturbed the Israeli people. They had never suffered such high losses before — nearly 3000 dead or missing out of a total population of under 3 million. Almost every family was affected. Their absolute confidence in the overwhelming superiority of their army and airforce was severely shaken. For most Israelis the war emphasized the need to keep defensible frontiers at all costs, though some saw it as an argument for greater efforts towards a permanent peace.

THE GOVERNMENT OF ISRAEL

Despite widespread criticism of the government's handling of the war, the ruling Labour Party weathered the storm and retained a majority in elections held in December 1973. Nevertheless, the Prime Minister, 75-year-old Mrs Golda Meir, and the Defence Minister, Moshe Dayan, the popular hero of the 1956 War, stepped down when a report on the conduct of the war was published.

The new Prime Minister was General Yitzhak Rabin, who had been Chief of Staff at the time of the 1967 War and later Israeli ambassador in Washington. Both he and his Foreign Minister, Yigael Allon, were willing to make some territorial concessions in order to achieve a settlement with the Arabs. Dr Kissinger returned to Israel and negotiated a second disengagement agreement between Israel and Egypt, signed in September 1975. His arrival in Israel, however, was greeted by violent demonstrations in Tel Aviv and Jerusalem, by Israelis who were opposed to further concessions.

Rabin never commanded the support he needed in the ruling coalition and his government remained weak. He was regarded as something of a "dove" in his attitude to the Arabs, while Shimon Peres, his rival and Minister of Defence was more of a "hawk". They clashed on many occasions, but particularly over the activities of the *Gush Emunim* (Bloc of the Faithful) movement, which sought the unrestricted right to establish Jewish settlements on the occupied West Bank, on the grounds that

45   Mrs Golda Meir, in 1969. She was Prime Minister of Israel from 1969 to 1974.

46   General Moshe Dayan, 1957. He was Chief of the Israeli General Staff between 1953 and 1958. He later entered politics and was Minister of Foreign Affairs in the Begin government from 1977 to his resignation in 1979.

the area belonged to historic Israel. In addition, the long mobilization of the Israeli reserve army and the need to re-equip and strengthen the armed forces created severe economic difficulties. Rabin was forced to introduce unpopular measures to curb inflation which cost him much support among the electorate, discouraged vitally important immigration, and did little to strengthen the economy. Early in 1977 scandals of corruption and bribery among politicians and in public life hit the Israeli headlines. Rabin himself was implicated, and he resigned as leader of the Labour Party.

The May 1977 election in Israel resulted in a surprise victory for the right-wing Likud party led by Menachem Begin, without doubt the "hawks" of Israeli politics. They won 43 out of the 120 seats in the Knesset — becoming the largest single party. People both inside and outside Israel were stunned by Begin's rise to power. Labour's defeat meant the end of an era in the history of Israel. It had been the Labour Party which led the Jewish settlers in Palestine after the 1930s and ruled continuously since the foundation of the state in 1948.

Labour's fall had begun with the 1973 war and the heavy death toll suffered. By 1977 two major shifts had occurred in the traditional party allegiances. A large number of oriental Jews (*Sephardim*), largely among the poorer and lower classes, voted for the Likud in protest against the failure of years of Labour government. At the same time many middle class western Jews (*Ashkenazim*), critical of Israel's policies over the occupied territories, Lebanon and Labour's scandals, or merely tired of war, voted for Yigael Yadin's newly formed Democratic Movement for Change. People voted against Labour, and Likud came to power because the votes were split among a number of smaller parties.

THE CAMP DAVID AGREEMENT

In November 1977 Begin publicly invited the Egyptian President to come to Jerusalem for peace talks. It must have been a profound shock when Sadat agreed. Sadat's visit to Jerusalem and his speech before the Israeli parliament (on 20 November 1977) was a spectacular gamble. By this dramatic gesture Sadat managed to get direct negotiations between Egypt and Israel under way. The negotiations which followed were long and complicated. Nevertheless, in September 1978, after the personal intervention of US President Jimmy Carter, a "Framework for Peace" was agreed by Begin and Sadat following talks at Camp David, the President's Maryland retreat. On 26 March 1979 a peace treaty between Israel and Egypt was signed in Washington by Sadat and Begin and witnessed by President Carter.

The treaty was almost entirely in Israel's favour. Israel had achieved its aim of a separate peace with Egypt, effectively neutralizing the only Arab state which posed a real threat to it, without making any significant commitment to autonomy for the inhabitants of the West Bank and Gaza. Israel gained the assurance of normal relations with Egypt, and even the prospect of buying Egyptian oil, and for this a withdrawal from Sinai and the dismantling of Israeli settlements there seemed a small price to pay. Begin made it abundantly clear that whatever Sadat might expect to the contrary, Israel would never return to the 1967 borders or permit the establishment of a Palestinian state. Nor would it return Jerusalem to Arab sovereignty.

ISRAEL AND THE OCCUPIED TERRITORIES

The Camp David agreement focused world attention once more on Israel's occupied territories. Since 1967 they have been subjected to military rule. Military governors enjoy a free hand in administration, and all rights of self-expression and political organization are denied to the Arab inhabitants. Those who refuse to collaborate are imprisoned or deported. Indeed, the occupation authorities have been criticized both inside and outside Israel for their harsh and repressive measures.

The refugees who were displaced during the 1967 war have been prevented from returning to their homes. Land belonging to Arab villages has been expropriated and new Jewish settlements established in growing numbers. In 1967 Prime Minister Golda Meir declared: "Jews have occupied the West Bank. For them to settle there for ever, the area must have the least

47 President Carter (centre) looks on as the Egyptian President Anwar Sadat and the Israeli Premier Menachem Begin put their signatures to the Egypt-Israel Peace Treaty in Washington on 26 March 1979.

48   Arab demonstrators light a street fire in Jerusalem in protest against the Israeli occupation.

possible number of Arabs". Areas like the West Bank have been gradually transformed in the twelve years of Israeli occupation and their resources, especially land, labour and water, have been firmly locked into the Israeli economy.

Following the Egyptian-Israeli treaty of March 1979, Prime Minister Begin made the Israeli position on the West Bank and Gaza quite clear:

> No Palestinian state shall be set up. No way. The Israeli army will have the job of preventing this. It is not just chance that the elected council is to have the title "administrative council". Administration and no more. We have offered autonomy and not sovereignty and the difference between the two is enormous.

Despite the provisions of the Camp David agreement, it soon became obvious that the autonomy being offered would give the Arab inhabitants very little real control over their own affairs. The systematic colonization and integration of the West Bank within the State of Israel was to be continued.

ISRAELI INTERVENTION IN SOUTHERN LEBANON

In 1977 fierce fighting erupted between Palestinian guerrillas and right-wing Christian militias in the area of southern Lebanon between the Litani river and the Israeli border. By the beginning of 1978 the Christian militias, led by Major Haddad and trained and supplied by Israel, were beginning to lose ground to the Palestinians and left-wing forces. Fearing the establishment of Palestinian guerrilla forces close to their northern border, the Israelis intervened. In March 1978, after Palestinian guerrillas attacked a bus near Tel Aviv in which 35 people were killed, a large-scale Israeli force invaded and occupied a border strip up to the Litani river in a search-and-destroy campaign against the Palestinians. The Israeli occupation left a trail of death and destruction. There were heavy civilian casualties, and a new wave of refugees fled during the shelling and aerial bombardments.

World reaction, and more important the reaction of America, was swift and severe. Israel was forced to withdraw after about three months, and a 6000 man UN force (UNIFIL) was stationed in southern Lebanon. But, in practice, Israel continued to control the border

"Sorry to interrupt any of your plans, but . . ."

49 In March 1978 a large Israeli force invaded southern Lebanon. When the Israelis withdrew three months later and a UN force was stationed there, they left behind a trail of death and destruction.

strip through her alliance with the Christian militias who had used the occupation to extend their activities and strengthen their forces. The UN presence could not prevent intensive Israeli air strikes against Palestinian bases and refugee camps, or new artillery barrages by both Israel and her Christian allies. These military actions devastated southern Lebanon, destroying towns and villages, and turning the border region into a virtual free-fire zone.

Faced with growing criticism at home and abroad for her military policies in southern Lebanon, the Israeli Government maintained that they were necessary to prevent Palestinian guerrilla raids inside Israel itself.

ISRAEL AND THE PALESTINIANS

The late Mrs Golda Meir, when she was Prime Minister of Israel, once asked the question "Who are the Palestinians?" They are the people displaced from their homes by the creation of the State of Israel in 1948 or living under Israeli occupation. The American-Jewish journalist

I.F.Stone, who covered the 1948 Arab-Israeli War as a reporter, later wrote: "It was a moral tragedy that in making a home for the remnants of the Holocaust we were drawn into a war in which we had to make a kindred people homeless, a people who had done us no harm."

Today there are about 3½ million people who call themselves Palestinians, a number almost equivalent to the present population of Israel. Some 500,000 of them live within Israel's pre-1967 borders, and about one million in the Israeli occupied territories of the West Bank and

50 Where the Palestinians live now : in total there are 3,528,000.

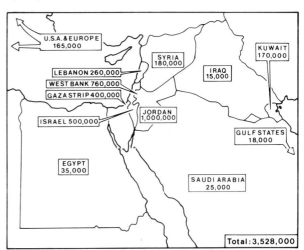

51 A vocational and teacher-training centre run by the United Nations Relief & Works Agency for Palestinian refugees at Ramallah on the West Bank.

Gaza. Of those who left their homeland, the majority found refuge in neighbouring Arab states, mainly in Jordan, Syria and Lebanon, while some sought employment in the oil-rich states of the Gulf and even outside the Middle East in western Europe, the USA and Latin America. Roughly 1½ million Palestinians are actually registered as refugees and just over one third, some 630,000 people, live in camps administered by the United Nations Relief and Works Agency (UNRWA). In its first report to the UN General Assembly in 1950 UNRWA stated:

> The desire to go back to their homes is general among all classes; it is proclaimed orally at all meetings and organized demonstrations, and, in writing, in all letters addressed to the Agency and all complaints handed in to the area officers. Many refugees are ceasing to believe in a possible return, yet this does not prevent them from insisting on it, since they feel that to agree to consider any other solution would be to show their weakness and to relinquish their fundamental right, acknowledged even by the General Assembly. They are, moreover, sceptical of the promised payment of compensation.

Nearly thirty years later many of the growing number of Palestinians, often with professional qualifications who have settled comfortably in a dozen different countries, still insist that their greatest desire is to "go home" to Palestine. Even the children of refugees who have never seen Palestine and those who left so young that they cannot remember it say the same thing. Many of those who fled from their homes can still produce the keys to their front doors and the deeds to their lands. It has frequently been said that the Palestinians hold the key to peace in the Middle East.

THE PALESTINIAN RESISTANCE GROUPS

In the aftermath of the 1948 Arab defeat and the upsurge of nationalist activity, the Palestinians believed that the liberation of their homeland could best be achieved by working with the Arab unity movement and by defeating imperialism and building strong Arab states. They resisted any rapprochement between Israel and the Arab states, fearing that this might lead to the final liquidation of the Palestinian cause. Efforts to reduce the plight of the Palestinians to merely a "refugee problem" were also firmly resisted. When the UN Secretary General formulated a plan to integrate the refugees into the economic life of the area in 1959, the Palestinians firmly rejected the idea and called on the Arab governments to oppose it.

As the movement for Arab unity lost momentum, several exclusively Palestinian organizations emerged, with the aim of mobilizing the Palestinian people to wage armed struggle against Israel. The most important of the organizations was *Al Fatah* (Arabic for *victory*) which was founded in 1956 as an underground organization. In 1959 it started issuing a limited circulation monthly, *Our Palestine*, which called on the Palestinians to take matters into their own hands and appealed to the Arab states to allow the Palestinian people to work for the liberation of their country. The turning point for Al Fatah came in March 1968 when a detachment of its commandos or *fedayeen*, under the command of regular units of the Jordanian army, held off a large Israeli strike force at the battle of Karameh in the Jordan valley. After the humiliation of the Six Day War, Karameh provided a huge boost for Arab morale and Fatah's strength rose rapidly to 10,000 regulars and several hundred militia. It was even forced to turn away volunteers. King Husain of Jordan himself was caught up in the general euphoria and declared "We are all fedayeen now". Fatah is generally regarded as the guerrilla group with the strongest power base among ordinary Palestinians. It does not believe in operations outside the Middle East

52   Three airliners, hijacked by the Popular Front for the Liberation of Palestine, were blown up before the world's television cameras at Dawson's Field, Jordan in September 1970.

and, publicly at least, dissociates itself from extremist groups like "Black September", responsible for the massacre of Israeli athletes at the Munich Olympics in 1972.

While Al Fatah describes itself as an Arab nationalist organization without any ideological slant, the second largest commando group is the Marxist Leninist Popular Front for the Liberation of Palestine (PFLP). Under its leader, the Christian-born Palestinian Dr George Habash, the PFLP, which emerged shortly after the 1967 war, attracted a hard core of young Palestinian graduates from middle-class families. The girl hijacker Leila Khalid was one of his recruits. The group's most spectacular exploit was the hijacking in September 1970 of US, British and Swiss airliners to an abandoned Second World War airfield in the Jordanian desert known as Dawson's Field. There, before the world's television cameras, the planes were blown up, though none of the passengers or crew were harmed. Two years later the PFLP hijacked a Lufthansa jumbo jet and collected five million dollars ransom for the plane and its passengers. The organization also has links with the notorious Japanese Red Army who attacked Israel's Lod international airport in May 1972, killing 26 people and wounding another 80.

In 1964, in an attempt to create a unified front, Al Fatah, the PFLP and the other resistance groups were brought together in the Palestine Liberation Organization (PLO). The PLO's executive committee, in which the various commando factions are represented, meets periodically to discuss issues of importance to the Palestine Resistance Movement as a whole. Its decisions are not binding, however, and the more revolutionary of the groups often ignore

them. Every year the PLO holds a meeting of the Palestine National Council, a Palestinian parliament set up by the Arab League in 1965. Since 1969, Al Fatah has been the dominant voice in the organization. Yasser Arafat, who became Chairman of the PLO in 1969, is a prominent member of the Al Fatah leadership. His success in maintaining at least a semblance of unity in the PLO is in itself a remarkable achievement.

KING HUSAIN OF JORDAN AND THE PALESTINIAN GUERRILLAS

The growth of the resistance movement was most spectacular in Jordan, where the majority of the population is Palestinian. Sporadic raids on Israel by Palestinian commandos based in Jordan provoked retaliatory raids by Israel against Jordan. After the Israelis raided the Jordanian village of Samu in November 1966, mass demonstrations swept the country. The Jordan government, too weak to hit directly back at Israel, unleashed a ferocious campaign of terror against the Palestinian organizations.

Despite this setback, the movement continued to grow and was strengthened after the Six Day War by its success at the battle of Karameh. The Palestinian resistance gradually took over the administration of the refugee camps in Jordan and began forming people's militias and councils. These activities were seen as a direct challenge to King Husain's regime, and a series of armed confrontations took place between Palestinian commandos and units of the Jordanian army. The King prepared for a decisive showdown. In what the Palestinians have come to call "Black September" 1970, the Bedouin troops of Jordan's royal army fought the fedayeen in heavy street fighting in Amman, the capital. It was estimated that at least 2000 commandos and Palestinian civilians were killed. After ten days of bloodshed mediation efforts by other Arab governments, and in particular by President Nasser, brought about a truce. Fighting flared up again in July 1971 when demoralized groups of commandos waded across the river Jordan and surrendered to Israeli patrols rather than remain in the Hashemite kingdom. From then on the Palestinian commandos were forced to shift the centre of their activity against Israel from Jordan to bases in Lebanon.

THE PALESTINIANS AND THE UNITED NATIONS

In September 1974 the UN agreed to debate "The Palestine Question" and included it on the agenda for the first time since 1948. Only four

53 Palestinian guerrillas, wearing the distinctive *kaffiyah* headgear, undergoing training on the Golan Heights.

54   One of the Palestinian refugee camps in Jordan which became the scene of fierce fighting between Palestinian commandos and regular units of the Jordanian army during "Black September" 1970.

governments were against this — Israel, the US, the Dominican Republic and Bolivia. In October 1974 the UN General Assembly voted to recognize the PLO as "the representative of the Palestinian people" and later that month the eighth Arab Summit Conference in Rabat, Morocco, proclaimed the PLO as "the sole legitimate representative of the Palestinian people": it had the right to speak for the Palestinians at any future Middle East peace talks and to establish an independent national authority in any part of Palestine which might be liberated from Israeli occupation.

On 13 November 1974 Yasser Arafat, Chairman of the PLO, addressed the UN General Assembly — the first time any Palestinian organization had taken part. In his speech he proposed the creation of a secular, democratic Palestinian state where Arabs and Jews could live together. In a memorable passage he said: 'I have come bearing an olive branch and a freedom-fighter's gun. Do not let the olive branch fall from my hand . . .". After this debate the UN passed Resolution 3236, recognizing the right of the Palestinians to self-determination, national independence and sovereignty. The PLO was also invited to take part in all future debates on the Middle East.

These decisions greatly strengthened the hand of the Palestinians, and of the PLO as their representatives. But the Israeli government adamantly refused to have any dealings with the PLO, dismissing it as a terrorist organization which Israel would meet "only on the battle-field". Following Yasser Arafat's appearance at the UN there were demonstrations on the West Bank in support of the PLO, to which the Israelis responded by arresting and deporting prominent Palestinians. Municipal elections organized by the Israeli occupation authorities in April 1976 demonstrated the strength of Palestinian nationalism and the widespread support enjoyed by the PLO among West Bank Palestinians. Unrest continued throughout 1976 and in December the UN General Assembly again condemned Israel's occupation policy. In February 1977 the UN Human Rights Commission expressed grave concern over the deteriorating situation in the occupied territories.

THE PALESTINIANS AFTER CAMP DAVID

Repeated declarations of the UN since 1974 and unrest on the West Bank highlighted the plight of the Palestinians and the Palestinian aspect of the Arab-Israeli conflict. The international standing of the PLO was greatly strengthened. The EEC countries stated their support for a Palestinian "homeland", as did the new US President, Jimmy Carter. By that time over a hundred states recognized the PLO. People were

67

55   Yasser Arafat, Chairman of the Palestine Liberation Organization, denounces the Egyptian-Israeli Peace Treaty at a training camp for Palestinian guerrillas outside Beirut (March 1979).

optimistic that there might at last be real progress on Palestinian self-determination. Then in November 1977 Sadat's initiative, followed by the Camp David agreements and the Egyptian-Israeli treaty signed in March 1979, threw the Arab world into confusion. The treaty offered the Palestinians of the West Bank and Gaza only a limited form of self-rule and this was criticized in the Arab World as being merely a formula for maintaining the Israeli occupation. Palestinians everywhere, the people no one asked, rejected the autonomy proposals. Yasser Arafat denounced the treaty as "a conspiracy". "What is being proposed", he said, "is a new form of slavery. Is there any village anywhere in the world where the inhabitants have no control over their water resources? But this is exactly what Begin is doing. What kind of autonomy is that, for example, which does not give us control of our drinking water?"

Behind the scenes the Americans, impatient with Israel's attitude at the autonomy talks and under pressure from Saudi Arabia, initiated a dialogue with the PLO. President Carter even went so far as to compare the Palestinian struggle for their rights with the American civil rights movement of the 1960s. But when it was disclosed that America's UN ambassador, outspoken black politician Andrew Young, had met unofficially with the PLO representative to

the UN, there was an uproar, especially among the Zionist lobby in Washington. After strident protests from Israel and the US Jewish community, Young was forced to resign. Despite this setback the PLO continued to gain popular support in the US, especially among the black community.

THE LEBANESE CRISIS

The State of Greater Lebanon, created by the French during the Mandate, was an artificial country. The largely Muslim population of the coastal areas of Beirut and Tripoli would have preferred to remain part of Syria. They felt a strong bond of solidarity with the Arab States of the Fertile Crescent and the Palestinians, and so contrasted strongly with the Maronite Christians of Mount Lebanon who were western orientated and had always fought to preserve their separate status within the Arab World. There was, therefore, no real bond of unity to hold the country and its people together in the face of economic and political difficulties.

When Lebanon became independent in 1943 an unwritten "National Pact" was agreed by the leaders of the various religious communities to share out between them the high offices of state and seats in the Assembly according to their numerical strength in the country. It was thus agreed that the President must always be a

Maronite, the Prime Minister a Sunni Muslim and the President of the National Assembly a Shi'a Muslim. Since the President and the Commander-in-Chief of the army were Maronites, they were in a position to ensure that their community retained a predominance which corresponded to their economic, educational and demographic superiority.

In many ways Lebanese society is feudal in character. The leaders of each community command unquestioning support (especially from the rural inhabitants), and in return they are expected to pass on the benefits of office through patronage and nepotism. Violence was always near the surface, and street fighting between communities in mixed villages not uncommon. But as social conditions began to change, traditional allegiances began to loosen. Nasser and the Socialist Arab revolutionary parties gained supporters among Lebanese who wanted to reform the old corrupt capitalist system and distribute wealth a little more evenly. As more and more people drifted to the cities, specially to Beirut, the capital, the traditional leaders no longer commanded their unquestioned support, and lost touch with their demands.

The rumblings of discontent were intensified by the tremendous disparity in wealth which emerged in the 1950s and 1960s. While four per cent of the population was very rich and getting visibly richer as the oil revenues from the Gulf flowed into Lebanon's banking and service economy, especially after 1973, the poor benefitted not at all. The government of Sulaiman Franjieh, elected in 1970, was more corrupt and partisan than was acceptable even to the Lebanese, and in some areas his administration failed to provide basic services such as water and electricity. In spite of calls for reform, the Maronites clung stubbornly to their entrenched position in the system. But, by the 1970s, large-scale emigration from their own community, coupled with the higher birth-rate of the Muslim population convinced them that they were no longer numerically the largest group, although they refused to hold a census in case it might be proved. The Muslims resented being under-represented and excluded from the benefits of the economic boom, though many of their leaders had a comfortable place in the Mafia-like system and did not attempt any reform.

The only real exception to this was Kamal Jumblatt, an extraordinary and complex character and the hereditary leader of the Druze Community. A feudal landowner with great personal wealth and the leading left-wing politician, Jumblatt was also an intellectual and a mystic who made occasional trips to India to see his guru. Over the years he established himself as the rallying point for the left and maintained friendly relations with the Palestinians, so that he emerged as one of the three or four most powerful men in the country.

These sources of discontent were pulling the fabric of Lebanese society apart, and the political leaders no longer represented the interests of the people, but only their own. This meant that people inevitably looked for other ways to bring about change.

THE PALESTINIANS IN LEBANON

The problems of the country were aggravated by the presence of large numbers of Palestinian refugees, and by the growing strength of the Palestinian Resistance movement. By 1975 Palestinians accounted for approximately one fifth of the Lebanese population.

The armed guerrilla factions amounted to a standing army which claimed sovereignty over the refugee camps and insisted on its rights to deal with the Palestinian bandits and gunmen who attacked Lebanese property. The Lebanese government was unable to deal with the problem because it knew that many Lebanese citizens were more sympathetic with the pan-Arab solidarity which the Palestinian resistance represented than they were committed to the existence of the Lebanon as a State. They feared, therefore, that they might provoke them into open revolt.

Israeli reprisals in response to Palestinian guerrilla attacks launched from South Lebanon increased and drove large numbers of poor Lebanese, mainly Shi'a Muslims, to swell the rootless, shifting population living in shantytowns and refugee-camps around Beirut. In these "belts of misery" radical and left-wing propagandists rapidly acquired supporters.

There had been outbreaks of fighting between Palestinians and Lebanese since 1967, but an Israeli raid on Beirut in 1973, which killed three Palestinian leaders, led to fierce battles between Palestinians and the Lebanese Army. President Franjieh did not dare to order an all-out attack on the guerrilla fighters, however, for fear of

provoking a mutiny.

The right-wing Christians, under the leadership of Pierre Gemayel, were afraid that the Palestinian resistance movement might draw Lebanon into a conflict with Israel that would compromise her neutrality and obliterate what they regarded as their "Christian" state. Their aim was to expel the Palestinians, and since the Lebanese Government appeared unwilling or unable to do it, they prepared to act themselves. President Franjieh's son, Tony, was a prominent leader of one of the Christian militias which they began to arm and train.

Alarmed at the build-up of militiamen and stockpiles of arms among the extreme right, the reformers and radicals of the left (by no means all Muslim) began to arm and train their own forces, obtaining arms from the Palestinians whom they had supported so steadily in the past.

CIVIL WAR IN LEBANON

When right-wing extremists attacked Palestinian forces in April 1975, the left-wing alliance came

56 Young Phalangists on patrol in Beirut, the shield of their machine gun decorated with pictures of the Virgin Mary.

to their defence. Although the Palestinian leaders maintained that they did not wish to interfere in Lebanese internal affairs, support for their presence became the criterion upon which people took sides once hostilities had broken out. The right-wing extremists, the *Kataeb* or Phalangists, saw the war as a struggle for the existence of their homeland, a western-oriented Christian state. The left-wing reformist alliance saw that there was no place for them in the sort of state which the Kataeb envisaged. Once the war had begun, the moderates and liberals on both sides were forced to adopt extreme positions for fear of their lives, and the population split largely according to confessional lines, that is, religious loyalties. Only Lebanon's Armenian community managed to retain a degree of neutrality, but eventually they too were engulfed in the hostilities.

The war, which started in Beirut but later infected the whole country, was characterized by its brutality and savagery. Individuals caught in the "wrong" territory were tortured, and

57   Just two of several hundred bodies lying dead in the Palestinian refugee camp of Tel az-Zaatar, Beirut after it fell to Christian forces in August 1976.

arge-scale massacres were committed by both sides, but if anything the Kataeb were the more brutal, acquiring world fame by their destruction of the Palestinian refugee-camp of Tel az-Zaatar.

The government rapidly lost control, for it was afraid to call in the army, whose loyalty was doubtful, and merely watched from the sidelines. The streets of Beirut were in the control of the militias and the city was soon effectively partitioned. Looters from both sides had a field-day in the prosperous city centre.

Syrian mediation produced yet another cease-fire in January 1976, but this too was shortlived, for it offered no real change in the previous system of government, and people had already suffered too much to be content with so little gain. Within a month full-scale war was resumed, fuelled by the mutiny of a Muslim officer,

Lieutenant Ahmed Khatib, who was soon followed by most of the lower ranks. The army split along confessional lines and took the war to the local garrisons all over the country. The Palestinians and the left-wing were in control of more or less two thirds of the country and were likely to win outright. President Franjieh refused to resign and fled to Jounieh, the "capital" of Christian-held Lebanon.

At this point Syria, traditionally a supporter of the Palestinian resistance and of Lebanese integration into the Arab World, changed sides. She feared the consequences of a Palestinian/left-wing victory: if a radical Palestinian regime were installed, it might provoke attack by Israel on Syria's most vulnerable frontier, when she was ill-prepared to defend herself; and if a critical left-wing government came to power it might stir Syria's own people into revolt. And so Syria ceased to supply arms and material support for the left-wing alliance, and secretly offered help instead to the Christian leaders.

Having made careful diplomatic preparations

71

to forestall international repercussions, Syria invaded Lebanon in May 1976, ostensibly to end the war. The Palestinian/left-wing alliance fought stubbornly and Syria proceeded slowly, unwilling to incite too much international controversy and denigration. In November 1976 Syrian troops occupied Beirut and the Palestinian forces withdrew to their bases in the south.

UNCERTAIN PEACE

Under Syrian tutelage, elections were held in Lebanon and a new government under Elias Sarkis, an experienced administrator, was returned to rebuild the shattered Lebanese economy. But the *de facto* partition of the country remains. Syrian and Arab forces are still necessary to separate the warring side and the basic problems remain unsolved. Israel intervention in the south against the Palestinian culminated in the invasion and temporary occupation of the border strip in March 1978 This, and Israel's continued support of right wing Christian militias, led by Major Haddad, in their attacks on both the United Nations peace keeping forces and the Palestinians, present a constant threat to the fragile peace. After months of fighting, the total destruction of the commercial centre of Beirut, on which the prosperity of the country rested, and something in the region of 60,000 deaths and 100,000 injured, little has been gained by either side. Life goes on, but the peace is fragile and often broken, and the underlying tensions and discontent remain.

YOUNG HISTORIAN

A

1 Who are the Palestinians?
2 Write a short paragraph on each of the various Palestinian resistance groups, outlining the differences between the more important ones.
3 Discuss the main causes of the Lebanese crisis of 1975.
4 What were the repercussions of the Yom Kippur War: (a) in Israel and (b) in the Arab States?
5 Why is so much importance attached to the occupied territories of the West Bank and the Gaza strip?
6 Assess the significance of Yasser Arafat's address to the United Nations General Assembly in 1974.
7 Why did Syria invade Lebanon in May 1976?
8 What were the main consequences of the Camp David agreements?

B

1 Imagine you are a refugee in a Palestinian refugee camp. Write a short account of life in the camp.

2 Write a newspaper article about Israel's capture of East Jerusalem in the Six Day War, (a) as an Israeli reporter, and (b) as an Arab reporter.
3 Write a newspaper report describing the movement of the Egyptian and Syrian forces in the Yom Kippur War. Illustrate your article with a sketch map.

C

1 Write the newspaper headlines which might have appeared above reports on: (a) "Black September" 1970; (b) the destruction of three airliners by Palestinian guerrillas at Dawson's Field in 1970; (c) the Israeli raid on Entebbe airport; (d) the election of Menachem Begin in May 1977; (e) the visit of President Sadat to Jerusalem in November 1977.

D

1 Draw three small sketch maps showing the territory covered by Israel, (a) in 1948; (b) after the Six Day War in 1967; (c) after the peace treaty with Egypt in 1979.

OIL POWER AND THE OIL STATES

OIL POWER AND POLITICS

The development of the Middle East oil industry has had a crucial impact on the political and economic history of the region since the beginning of the twentieth century and, in particular, since the Second World War. Oil revenues have financed the economic transformation of the oil-producing countries. At the international level, the Middle East occupies a central place in the growing energy crisis of an oil-hungry world.

MIDDLE EAST OIL

At the beginning of the twentieth century oil supplied only 4 per cent of the world's energy requirements, while 90 per cent came from coal. Oil exploration began in the Middle East in 1901 when William Knox d'Arcy was granted the first oil concession in Iran. Oil was eventually discovered in Iran in 1908 and later in Iraq (1923), Bahrain (1932), Saudi Arabia (1937), Kuwait (1938) and Qatar (1940). More recently oil exploitation has involved Algeria, Libya and Abu Dhabi (1958), Oman (1963) and Dubai (1965). Industrial development in western Europe and Japan since the Second World War resulted in a dramatic increase in oil consumption. As a comparatively cheap and versatile source of energy, oil rapidly replaced other more traditional sources of energy. By the 1970s oil had become essential to the maintenance of

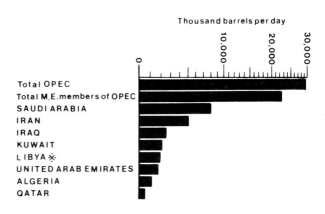

Thousand barrels per day

58　Crude oil production of the Middle East members of OPEC in 1979 (thousand barrels per day).
*Socialist People's Libyan Arab Jamahiriyah.

the modern way of life in most of the western world. No alternative source of energy of comparable quality being available in the short term, the industrialized countries must probably remain dependent on oil resources for the foreseeable future.

The Middle East became an increasingly important oil supplier. Although oil production began in the early part of the twentieth century, output rose rapidly only after the Second World War. In the 1930s less than 5 per cent of world oil was supplied by the Middle East. By 1965 the region produced more than one quarter of world supplies and by the late 1970s almost one half. In 1978 Japan obtained 74 per cent of her oil imports from the Middle East, western Europe 79 per cent and the United States 43 per cent. Proven oil reserves are also highly concentrated in the Middle East. An estimated two thirds of known oil reserves outside the Soviet

73

59 The vast storage tanks of Saudi Arabia's major oil refinery at Ras Tanura. Saudi Arabia is the major Middle Eastern oil producer and alone contains one quarter of the world's oil reserves.

Bloc are located in this region. Saudi Arabia contains the largest reserves of any single country in the world and is by far the major Middle East oil producer. This level of concentration has led to very high dependence by industrialized countries on the oil supplies and reserves of the Middle East.

REVOLUTION IN OIL POWER

Until 1972 oil exploration and production in the Middle East was mainly carried out by western oil firms. They held concessions, mostly granted in the 1920s and 1930s, giving them exclusive rights for the exploration and development of petroleum resources. These concessions often covered whole countries and were usually granted for periods of 50–75 years. They were in effect "states within a state". In the 1920s and 1930s seven major oil companies dominated the region's oil industry. These powerful companies, popularly known as the "Seven Sisters", were Exxon (Esso), Royal Dutch Shell, Texaco, Standard Oil of California, Mobil, Gulf and British Petroleum. Oil production started to increase rapidly in the 1940s. Realizing the

74

potential of their resources, oil-producing countries began to seek higher returns from oil sales than they were receiving under the existing system of royalty payments. The neocolonial mode of operation adopted by the companies brought the concession system under attack and the oil-producing countries began to demand greater control over oil supplies and oil production.

The first major change in the Middle East occurred in 1950 when Saudi Arabia, Kuwait and Iraq, following the precedent established by Venezuela in 1948, introduced a system of profit sharing. The "50-50 profit split", as it became known, divided revenues equally between the government and the company. In 1951 a nationalist government came to power in Iran and took a more daring initiative when it nationalized the Anglo-Iranian Oil Company. The western powers in reply applied strong political and economic pressure on the Iranian government and Iranian oil was effectively boy-cotted on world markets. The resulting collapse of her economy and the halt in oil exports forced Iran to negotiate a new agreement in 1954. The state-controlled National Iranian Oil Company, which had been set up in 1951, was forced to compromise by granting what amounted to a new concession to the newly formed "Iranian Consortium", which replaced the Anglo-Iranian Oil Company and was composed of the major western oil companies. The terms of the concession included the principle of the 50-50 profit split. The first attempt at the nationalization of Middle East oil had failed.

Oil concessions granted in the 1950s and 1960s were more beneficial to the host countries. Smaller areas were granted, and the length of concessions was restricted. From 1957 host countries also demanded state participation in concessions and in some cases a 75-25 profit split was agreed. In 1966 Iran further increased state participation by introducing a system of service contracts. Under this system, Iran retained ownership of oil which was discovered, but offered contracts for oil development and oil export sales.

The most far-reaching agreement for the modification of existing concessions was the General Agreement of 1972. The principle of state participation in existing concessions was firmly endorsed and oil-producing countries were entitled to an immediate stake of 25 per cent of company concessions. This stake was scheduled to rise to 51 per cent by 1982, giving producing countries the majority share. In Iraq, however, the principle of joint participation was rejected and in 1972 the Iraq Petroleum Company was nationalized outright. In 1973 the entire Iranian oil industry was once more nationalized, and both Kuwait and Qatar later took over complete ownership of their oil-producing operations. On the other hand, in Saudi Arabia and Abu Dhabi, where large reserves are still to be brought into production, participation agreements survived, although the government share rose to 60 per cent. Even with nationalization, the major western oil companies still control the transportation and distribution of oil to world markets and their influence remains considerable.

THE ORGANIZATION OF PETROLEUM EXPORTING COUNTRIES (OPEC)

Partly because of increased state control over the oil industry, governments became aware that oil was under-priced on the world market. OPEC, the Organization of Petroleum Exporting Countries, was established in 1960 and now contains all the major Middle East oil producers, together with Venezuela, Indonesia, Nigeria, Ecuador and Gabon. Initially the new organization pressed in vain for an increase in oil prices. By 1970, however, the oil supply situation had tightened and in 1971 in Tehran, the Iranian capital, the "Seven Sisters" and six Gulf producers agreed to an immediate price rise. It was decided that prices were to rise in line with inflation in the future. Instability of the American dollar, coupled with increased

60 The Saudi Arabian delegation, headed by Oil Minister Zaki Yamani (third from left), and that of the United Arab Emirates, headed by Mana Saeed Al-Otaiba (second from right), at a meeting of the Organization of Petroleum Exporting Countries held in Vienna in March 1974.

Don't just sit there!
~ Lose some weight!

WEST

RECESSION

61　In 1979 the OPEC oil producers became more reluctant to increase the supply of oil to the west and insisted that the industrialized nations limit their consumption. One of the main lessons of the Iranian revolution for other Middle East producers was that fast spending financed by high rates of oil production can be socially destabilising.

demand for oil by the United States, resulted in further price increases within a few months of the Tehran agreement. This round of price rises triggered the unprecedented increases in the cost of oil announced in October 1973. Prices quadrupled and the western economies entered a period of recession and mounting unemployment. In the Third World, with its already low standard of living, the consequences were even more serious.

OPEC became an all-powerful body, determining the price of the world's oil. But divisions emerged within it about the extent to which oil prices should rise. Saudi Arabia, led by its powerful Oil Minister, Shaikh Yamani, attempted to restrict price increases, while countries such as Libya and Iraq pressed for much higher levels. Despite these differences of opinion, by the early 1970s OPEC had consolidated its position as an impressive cartel with strong bargaining powers affecting both the prices and quantities of world oil supplies.

OIL REVENUES

The advent of the oil era, coupled with changes in ownership and rising oil revenues, brought fabulous wealth to the oil-producing countries. Oil changed the political map of the Arabian Peninsula. Both on-shore and off-shore political boundaries had to be precisely drawn and disputes were not uncommon. New or revised political systems also developed to deal with the new-found wealth. From 1973 oil revenues increased dramatically. They were used to undertake ambitious development plans, or for the lavish provision of social services, or they were merely squandered according to the whims

62　Heavy manual work in the Gulf states is performed almost entirely by migrants, many from the Indian subcontinent.

of autocratic rulers. The wealth of the oil-rich states has created contrasts in the degree of modernization and development between the "haves" and the "have nots" of the Middle East. New wealth and the military strength and political influence which oil riches could buy gave the oil producers, and Saudi Arabia in particular, a decisive role in Middle Eastern affairs.

THE OIL WEAPON

As a result of growing world dependence on Middle Eastern oil, by the early 1970s the Arab oil producers began to realize that oil could be used as a powerful weapon of diplomacy, especially to bring pressure on the USA and other western nations to moderate their pro-Israeli policy in the Middle East. In 1956, following the Suez crisis, oil supplies to western Europe were cut off but with no significant effect. In 1968 the Organization of Arab Petroleum Exporting Countries (OAPEC) was set up to safeguard the interests of Arab oil states and to determine ways of strengthening their co-operation in the petroleum industry. OAPEC also attempted to influence the behaviour of oil consumers. The strength of the oil weapon was demonstrated by the events following the 1973 Arab-Israeli war. October 1973 was not only a milestone because of the dramatic oil price rises, it also marked the first use of oil power as a political weapon.

Soon after the outbreak of the war, there were calls within the Arab world for measures to deny Middle East oil to the supporters of Israel. On 17 October a meeting in Kuwait of representatives of the Arab oil producers resulted in an agreement to reduce output. Two days later Abu Dhabi took the lead in stopping all oil exports to the United States. Initial production cuts of 5 per cent were soon increased to 25 per cent and the screw tightened. The effects were soon evident. On 6 November the EEC countries endorsed a statement calling for an Israeli withdrawal from the territories occupied in 1967 and acknowledging the rights of the Palestinians. This provoked accusations from Israel that the Europeans were giving in to "Arab blackmail". Without doubt, the oil weapon will be used in the future to achieve both political and economic aims.

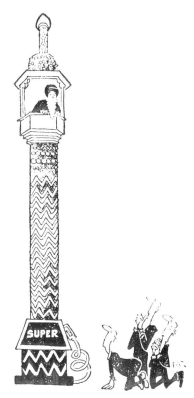

(Dessin de PLANTU.)

63 In 1979 the reduction in the supply of oil which resulted from the Iranian revolution was not as big as it was at the height of the Arab embargoes at the end of 1973, but it led to a new world oil crisis.

OIL POWER IN LIBYA

Libya, under its charismatic leader, Colonel Gaddafi, was the first Middle East oil producer to adopt a new mood of militancy in its relations with the international oil companies in the early 1970s. Libya was a late starter in the oil race — the oil boom did not get under way until 1961 — and as a result the structure of its oil industry was very different from that in Saudi Arabia, Iran or Iraq. There, a single major oil company enjoyed a virtual monopoly over oil exploration and production. But in Libya a large number of small independent oil companies held concessions. Through their efforts and the highly competitive terms under which concessions were granted, the Libyan oil industry grew at an unprecedented rate. Libya was the first country to surpass production of one million barrels a day in less than five years from the start of production. By 1968 Libya was supplying more than one third of western Europe's oil imports. Some of the independent companies were heavily dependent on Libya for the bulk of their oil supplies; one of the leading independents, Occidental, obtained 97 per cent of all its output from Libya. Instead of Libya relying on the oil companies, the reverse was the case. After 1969 the vulnerability of the independent operators was fully exploited by the new Gaddafi regime, which felt a blazing sense of persecution at the hands of foreign oil monopolies and was prepared to adopt tough tactics in the tortuous world of oil politics. When Libya moved to spearhead OPEC's early push for price increases in 1970-71, its independent operators gave in, one after another, forcing the major companies to follow suit for fear of losing their concessions. Libya also led those oil producers who demanded participation in oil company activities. From 1977 foreign oil interests in Libya had to work in cooperation with the state-owned National Oil Company which has gradually acquired majority shares in all local operations, together with those concessions that were entirely taken over — as, for example, BP's Libyan interests. These were nationalized in 1971 in retaliation for the British government's failure to prevent the Iranian occupation of the Gulf islands of Abu Musa and the Tumbs. The Libyan government's share of oil revenues soared, so that the country's income from oil in the late 1970s averaged $8000 million. The level of GNP per capita rose to $6680 — making Libya, with under 3 million inhabitants, one of the richest states in the world.

GADDAFI AND THE LIBYAN REVOLUTION

The discovery of oil transformed Libya from rags to riches, but under King Idris, who ruled from independence in 1951 until the military take-over in 1969, the country remained a client state of western interests. Its government was in the hands of corrupt tribal notables; the people were demoralized. Both Britain and the USA maintained huge military bases on Libyan soil. Nationalist stirrings finally burst forth from below the surface on 1 September 1969, when the king was deposed by a military coup. The coup was organized by young army officers led by a 27-year-old colonel, Muammar Gaddafi.

64   Colonel Gaddafi.

It was a copy book coup. In a matter of hours a small group of audacious young men overthrew the government and seized control of the state, with minimum deployment of forces and almost no bloodshed. Most of the new men of the revolution were from poor families from the interior who had joined the army because there were no other outlets or opportunities for them. Gaddafi himself was born in Sirte, in the desert that reaches to the coastline between Tripolitania and Cyrenaica. His family, he claims, still live in a tent, and he spent his formative years in the oasis town of Sebha in the Fezzan.

The coup released a wave of popular enthusiasm among the Libyan people, but from the outset supreme power lay with the 12-man Revolutionary Command Council (RCC), hand-picked by Gaddafi, its chairman. He also became the head of government and commander-in-chief of the army. The RCC worked round the clock, generally from the Azzizia barracks near Tripoli where Gaddafi took up residence and which the Council made its headquarters. The new regime banned all political parties, nationalized foreign businesses and took over the British and American military bases. Emphasis was laid on the importance of the Arabic language and a return to the fundamental precepts of Islam in everyday life. Development programmes initiated under the monarchy were speeded up and greatly expanded. Schools,

78

hospitals and clinics were built throughout the country and opened to all, free of charge. A massive effort was made to provide better housing and rows of new flats and small houses replaced the slums and shanty towns which grew up in the 1960s. Above all, the young officers strove to give the Libyans new self-respect, by erasing from their memories the humiliation they had felt at the hands of the contemptuous Italian colonizers and other foreigners.

Gaddafi, the undisputed leader of the revolution, maintained that the revolution stood for what benefitted the people, and people's power became the recurring theme of his frequent public speeches. Yet, to those who pressed for democratic institutions, Gaddafi declared that the young officers of the revolution, the sons of poor families, were the people and therefore their power meant power to the people.

In the 1970s Gaddafi developed his own ideas as to how the transformation of Libyan society should be carried out. He published them in his famous Green Book. Opposed to both capitalism and communism, Gaddafi wanted to try to develop an intermediate system in Libya — his so-called Third Theory. In the book Gaddafi is critical of the traditional forms of western democracies and party systems, and maintains

65   Poster showing Libyan workers demanding the replacement of an idle official. In reality, popular enthusiasm for "people's power" never reached the level of revolutionary fervour portrayed either in the numerous posters or in Gaddafi's own statements.

66   Under Gaddafi's rule, major new housing projects have been completed throughout the country.

that only the establishment of popular congresses can ensure full participation of the masses in decision-making. Ordinary citizens constitute the popular base of the pyramid. They should form basic popular congresses throughout the country and send delegates to the people's committees and various professional and union organizations which in turn should send delegates to the General People's Congress (GPC). The GPC would then elect a General Popular Committee to replace the Council of Ministers. Each section of the Committee would be managed by a Secretary. The highest organ of the pyramid would be a General Secretariat replacing the Revolutionary Command Council. By delegation and not by representation, Gaddafi argues, power would remain at grass-roots in the hands of the people.

These ideas were put into practice in March 1977 when Gaddafi proclaimed the advent of direct people's power and changed Libya's name to the Libyan Arab Socialist People's Jamahiriya (the word Jamahiriya derives from the Arabic *jamahir* which means the people or masses). Assessments of Gaddafi's latest political experiment varied. Regarded by some as a gigantic fraud to disguise Gaddafi's continuing dictatorial rule, it was seen by others as a sincere attempt to overcome the inertia and passivity of the Libyan people and involve them in the country's government. Certainly Libya is still a long way from achieving its elusive revolution.

GADDAFI'S FOREIGN POLICY

Gaddafi emerged as one of the world's most outspoken leaders, attacking both friend and foe with equal righteousness and pursuing an active if, at times, seemingly erratic foreign policy. When he came to power, the Arab world was more deeply divided than ever. Egypt had been defeated in the 1967 war with Israel, more Arab lands had been occupied, and Arab ranks were in disarray. It was Gaddafi's deeply held belief that every setback to the Arab cause arose from Arab disunity. The Arab world had to be united to win the battle for Palestine. Therefore, the vision of one Arab nation from the Gulf to the Atlantic, opposition to Zionism and to its ally, western imperialism, became the dominant themes in Libya's foreign relations.

Almost immediately Gaddafi suggested that Libya form an alliance with Egypt and Sudan in a revolutionary front to consolidate three progressive revolutions. The Tripoli Charter linking the three countries was signed in December 1969. Gaddafi pressed for complete unity between the three states but President Nasser of Egypt, mindful of the collapse of the Egyptian-Syrian union, was more cautious. After Nasser's death the three states, now joined by Syria, translated their projected merger into a union. In April 1971 the Federation of Arab Republics comprising Egypt, Libya and Syria was founded, on the principles of no negotiated peace with Israel and no slackening of support for the Palestinian cause. In Sudan left-wing groups strongly objected to the union and mounted a coup in July 1971 which the President, Nimeiry, succeeded in crushing only with Libyan and Egyptian help. Yet far from strengthening Sudan's commitment to the new Federation, Nimeiry's return to power threw Sudan towards the other Arab axis which had been formed between Saudi Arabia and the Gulf states under United States protection. The Federation generated a lot of paper but no action and its institutions lacked real power. Its shortcomings convinced Gaddafi that something closer and stronger was needed.

In July 1972 Gaddafi called for an immediate merger of Egypt and Libya, and an agreement was signed to take effect in September 1973. For Nasser's successor, Sadat, the merger was just one more bid to buy time and, as the date for union drew nearer, he appeared to hesitate. Gaddafi became increasingly impatient and in July 1973 despatched 40,000 Libyans towards Cairo on a "unity march" designed to pressure Sadat into bringing about the immediate fusion of the two countries. The marchers were turned back at the frontier and relations between the two states quickly deteriorated. When Egypt declared war on Israel in October 1973, Gaddafi, who had been the strongest supporter of the Palestinian movements, the chief paymaster of the *fedayeen* and the leading advocate of war with Israel, was not consulted. He was deeply offended and since then there has been an almost unbroken propaganda war between the two countries. In July 1977 the war of words flared briefly into armed clashes between Egyptian and Libyan forces. Following President Sadat's peace initiatives, which were bitterly denounced by Libya, Gaddafi renewed his appeal for Arab unity, arguing that the Egyptian-Israeli treaty must be nullified by concerted

Arab action against Israel. Arab backing for Libya was also sought, to warn President Sadat against any further military adventures on the Libyan frontier.

Gaddafi's much publicized African policy, like his call for Arab unity, formed part of his scheme to liberate Arab lands from Zionist aggression. He believed that Israel's presence in Africa threatened the Arab states through their own backdoor. Employing a policy of religious propaganda and promises of financial assistance and aid, Libya appealed to her Black African, largely Muslim neighbours to sever their diplomatic relations with Israel. This policy achieved some notable successes, but it also

drew Libya into a disastrous involvement with Amin's brutal and repressive regime in Uganda.

Gaddafi's support for such movements as the Irish Republican Army (IRA) can be seen as aimed at "British imperialism", and so can his aid to nearby Malta. Towards the end of the 1970s, however, Gaddafi tried to exert influence by seeking the role of mediator between various Muslim minorities which he previously supported and their respective governments, notably in the Philippines and Chad. These were signs, some observers believed, of a new spirit of moderation and reconciliation in Gaddafi's often turbulent and unpredictable foreign relations.

YOUNG HISTORIAN

A

1 Explain what was meant by oil concessions. What were the differences between concessions granted before 1950, and those after?

2 Write a short account of the following: (a) the General Agreement of 1972; (b) OPEC; (c) the Tehran Agreement of 1971.

3 What were the effects of the 1973 increase in oil prices?

4 Give examples of how Middle Eastern oil states have used their wealth.

5 Outline the growth of the oil industry in Libya.

6 Why does President Gaddafi believe in Arab unity and how has this influenced his policies?

7 Assess how successful President Gaddafi's policy in Africa has been.

B

1 Imagine you are an adviser to President Gaddafi. Outline what you see as the advantages of unification between Libya and Egypt.

C

1 Write the newspaper headlines which might have appeared above reports on: (a) the nationalization of British oil interests in Libya; (b) the quadrupling of Middle Eastern oil prices in 1973; (c) the "unity march" of 40,000 Libyans to Cairo in July 1973.

D

1 Draw a map of Middle Eastern oil-producing countries, indicating the dates when oil was discovered.

PRESENT-DAY PROBLEMS - DIFFERENT PERSPECTIVES

Today most countries in the world, whether they are big or small, find themselves directly affected by what is happening in the Middle East. Oil, which the Arabs possess and the rest of the world badly needs, is one important factor. Another is the violence that has characterized various stages of the conflict between the Arabs and Israel. Many countries around the world have been forced to adopt a specific stand or role on this explosive issue, at the United Nations and elsewhere. Between 1967, when the Arabs suffered a humiliating defeat, and 1977, when President Sadat of Egypt went to Jerusalem, the Middle East crisis occupied the minds of most world leaders and the interest of ordinary people across the world. Many people in the west still remember the oil embargo of 1973. During this period strife-torn Lebanon was equally in the minds of many people, and hijackings and the destruction of aircraft on the ground are not easily forgotten. But, above all, the energy squeeze, rising oil prices and the world recession have affected the peoples of rich and poor countries alike.

THE SUPERPOWERS

The attitudes of the two superpowers to developments in the Middle East are of overwhelming importance. Both America and Russia evolved their own policies towards the region, based on their view of local interests and problems but also based on their relations with each other in a more global perspective.

The decline of British power and influence in the Middle East after the Second World War led the USA to assume greater responsibility for security in the region against what they saw as the threat of Soviet penetration. During the Cold War period of the 1950s and 60s the Americans did their best to organize those Middle East countries who were friendly towards them into pacts, to guard the area against the expansionist tendencies of the Soviet Union. More recently the end of the Cold War and the global considerations of *détente* between the two superpowers have brought about changes in American policy towards the Middle East. Advances in missile technology and satellite surveillance have reduced the need for Americans to construct and maintain military bases within the region. In place of direct intervention, local allies such as Israel, Iran and, since the downfall of the Shah, Egypt, have been groomed as policemen to protect US interests.

Since the early 1970s security of American oil supplies from the Middle East has become the central theme of American policy towards the region. By 1979 the US imported half its daily oil consumption. This fact led to a serious conflict of interest between America's traditional support for Israel, to satisfy the powerful Jewish lobby in Washington, and her need to adopt a more "even-handed" approach to her relations with the Arab States. In fact, the separate peace treaty between Egypt and Israel, masterminded by US President Jimmy Carter, alienated even America's conservative allies, Saudi Arabia and Jordan. With anti-American feeling running high in Iran's new Islamic Republic and America's special relationship with Saudi Arabia undermined, the threat to vital oil supplies must appear more real than ever to US leaders. There have even been thinly disguised warnings that America might use military force to protect the

67 American/Middle East friendship. US President Carter (left) with President Assad of Syria, 1977.

oil-fields if necessary.

Unlike the USA, the Soviet Union does not possess the same extensive and deep-rooted economic presence in the Middle East because it lacks the global economy of its co-superpower. In their early days in the Middle East the Soviet Union backed the Arab communist parties, but it soon became clear that the communists were not going to win power. The Russians therefore switched their support to the nationalist leaders, adopting the convenient doctrine of "revolutionary nationalism". When the nationalists suppressed the communist parties, the Russians told the latter to disband and infiltrate themselves into the single-party governments of the nationalists.

In the late 1950s the Iraqi revolution and Nasser's struggle against Britain and France made it appear virtually certain to the Soviet Union that the Arab States were going to swing, one after the other, from unpopular monarchies to left-wing revolutionary leadership under Soviet guidance, and soon after to government by the Arab communist parties. But Russian hopes that the communists would be able to work their way to power were not fulfilled. Russia discovered that backing the nationalists had the disadvantage that their

regimes were not under Soviet control, and Arab leaders quickly learnt how to play off one superpower against the other. In Iraq the communists overplayed their hand and were suppressed by Kassem whose position they had threatened. The monarchies of Saudi Arabia and Jordan showed unexpected strength and resilience; and in spite of all the Soviet arms flooding into Egypt, Nasser was soundly beaten by the Israelis in the Six Day War.

After Nasser's death the new trends accelerated. The communist coup against Nimeiry in Sudan was quickly suppressed by joint Egyptian and Libyan action; President Sadat sent away almost all the Soviet advisers in Egypt and the facilities for the Soviet Navy and Airforce were terminated. Even the October War of 1973 had only a limited effect in favour of the Egyptian-Soviet connection, and it was not long before President Sadat turned instead to the United States and Europe to make good the arms which he had lost and to Henry Kissinger to help him begin the long and difficult negotiations to secure the removal of Israeli forces from Egyptian territory. At the same time the quadrupling of oil prices enabled Saudi Arabia and the Gulf rulers to give financial support to the less-favoured Arab states, until in 1976 the Soviet leaders were forced to witness the Syrians, financed by Saudi Arabia, using Soviet arms against left-wing Palestinians.

Soviet policy-makers were forced into opportunism, dictated by often conflicting developments. Increasingly their reaction to Middle Eastern issues was determined by the requirements of their general policy, in particular their relations with the Americans in the nuclear field. This forms the basis of their foreign policy and one of the most important reasons for their policy of *détente*.

Nevertheless the Russians are anxious to increase their influence in a region which Krushchev once described as "our own backyard". And, by virtue of being a co-superpower, the Russians' reaction to American policy initiatives on the Middle East cannot be ignored in Washington. Without Soviet help, Egypt could never have inflicted the damage on Israel which it did in 1973; and many observers believe that, without Soviet leader Brezhnev's celebrated warning to President Carter in November 1978, the US would probably have intervened militarily in Iran. Arab opposition to the American-backed Egyptian-Israeli Peace Treaty, a weakening of the special relationship between the US and

83

68   The Turkish Prime Minister, Bülent Ecevit (third from right) arrives in Moscow on an official visit, 1978.

Saudi Arabia and consequently an improvement in Soviet relations with that country opened up new opportunities during 1980 for Moscow to re-establish its position as a friendly power in the region. But the Soviet Union is wary and unlikely to risk a confrontation with America in the Middle East.

Whatever changes occur in American and Russian perspectives on the Middle East, their role remains of paramount importance for the future of the region. Recent events have demonstrated only too clearly that no lasting and peaceful solution to the region's outstanding problems can be found without the agreement and cooperation of both the world's superpowers.

DISILLUSIONMENT AND FRUSTRATION

Seen from outside, the Middle East is often portrayed as a region of chronic instability and endemic conflicts, and yet at the same time as a treasure-house containing the major source of one of the world's most valuable and sought-after commodities — oil. For the peoples living in the Middle East the perspectives are different, and other issues are dominant and deeply felt.

For many of them, governing themselves and trying to catch up with the technological progress of the west has brought disillusionment and intolerable frustration. Growing contact with the modern world since the late nineteenth century made them realize only too clearly just how far behind they had fallen in the march of civilization. Their political leaders turned away from Islam, which more than anything else had shaped Middle Eastern society and institutions over thirteen centuries, and embraced western ideas of secular nationalism. Religion, if not rejected outright, was seen as a barrier to progress, the opium of the masses.

After the First World War and the political fragmentation imposed by the European colonialist powers, there was a rush to imitate those European-style institutions which they believed would eventually make them strong. Later, after the Second World War, when most countries secured at least a nominal independence, many were carried away by various revolutionary doctrines designed to modernize their societies. The most influential of these were Nasserism and Baathism which both adopted slogans of "Unity", in order to complete the process of liberation from domination by the western powers, and "Socialism", the vehicle of material progress and social justice. These imported ideologies, by which the Middle East tried to confront the western challenge in western terms, failed abysmally. Political leaders and intellectuals failed to adapt them to the cultural and historical setting or put them in language which the mass of the people could really understand. Baathism,for instance, quickly degenerated into a mouthing of mechanical slogans and dogmas. Almost everywhere imported institutions were turned into instruments for the preservation of power and the enrichment of political élites at the expense of the majority of the citizens.

In the 1970s oil added a new dimension. In theory, growing wealth from oil should have strengthened the Arab States as the new wealth gave them the potential for economic development and for increasing their political influence in the world. In practice, far from solving their problems, oil wealth in many cases merely aggravated long-established corruptions and widened the gap between rich and poor.

There has been no more humiliating reminder of the widespread disillusionment and frustration than the famous peace mission of Sadat. In the west it was applauded and Sadat and Begin were awarded the Nobel Peace Prize. For the Arabs it illustrated the bankruptcy of the whole post-independence revolutionary struggle; for here was the heir of Nasser trying to make peace with Begin, the embodiment of Zionism at its most expansionist and extreme.

ETHNIC IDENTITY
AND ETHNO-NATIONALISM

The constitutional revolution of Reza Shah, the Atatürk reforms and above all the rise of pan-Arab secular nationalism at the turn of the last century, all contributed to create a new concept of citizenship in the Middle East. The old codes of privilege and segregation, formalized by the Ottoman millet system, were replaced by the standardized laws of the modern states. More recently, the profound social and economic changes introduced by oil wealth and modern technology have all but abolished the former occupational specialization of minorities along ethnic lines; no longer are Armenians identified with crafts, Jews with money lending, Copts with the civil service and Circassians with the Police. Today it is easier for an Armenian to become Arab, but much more difficult to remain Armenian — that is, to retain his separate ethnic identity.

But this process of social change is nowhere near completion. Even the most modernizing regimes have encountered resistance in attempting to transform their citizens along lines that transcend ethnic affiliation. In Turkey, Egypt, Syria and Tunisia, states with probably the most advanced social legislation in the Middle East, categories of social class and party allegiance are still struggling to emerge as the dominant expression of social identity and political consciousness. The spirit of millet regulations in different guises has survived in the Personal Status codes, the various ecclesiastical courts and the extra-legal channels of ethnic nepotism — down to the "minorities' quotas" which are an open secret in many Middle Eastern government employment bureaux and university admission offices. Lebanon provides the most extreme example of the contradiction which has arisen between the official view of a unified citizenry and the heritage of the millet system.

Serveral national minorities, however, seek to reverse the dominant trend by strengthening their ethnic identity in the direction of a separate national consciousness. The Maronites of the Lebanon, the peoples of the southern Sudan, and the Kurds yearn for independence or autonomy.

Of all the national minorities in the Middle East the Kurds are perhaps the most distinct in terms of their national consciousness and preservation of traditional culture. Their national aspirations were rejected when the European

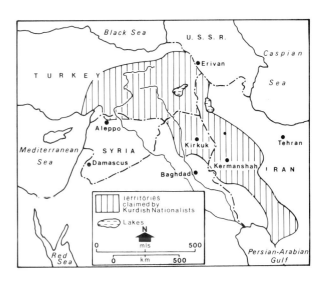

69   Kurdish territorial claims.

70 A series of Kurdish revolts in northern Iraq have provoked harsh reprisals from the central government in Baghdad. The Kurdish population have suffered severely but they remain staunchly independent and have retained their national consciousness.

powers carved up the territories of the defeated Ottoman Empire at the end of the First World War. The Kurds found themselves divided between six different states and hardly referred to as a people. Only Iraq and the USSR recognize their separate identity. In Turkey, for example, there is an official ban on making references to the "Kurdish people" in the press and party platforms. The teaching of the Kurdish language is forbidden by law in both Iran and Turkey, and in Iraq, despite the Kurdish Autonomy Law of 1974, there is an effective policy of Arabization in designated Kurdish areas. Kurdish nationalism has been forced underground. In Iraq and Iran Kurdish discontent has erupted in a number of full-scale revolts which have been brutally crushed by central government forces, but no united Kurdish struggle for nationhood has proved possible.

THE ISLAMIC REVIVAL

The 1970s witnessed a remarkable Islamic revival experienced throughout the Middle East and beyond it. Outward expressions of the growing strength of Islam are found at both official and popular levels. The most striking indications include the banning of alcohol, the enforcing of more modest apparel for women and the reappearance of headcovering if not the veil. Many politicians now call for the re-introduction of the Sharia or Islamic law, even in states where religion has been officially played down in the past in favour of militant nationalism. The leader of Egypt's left-wing opposition party recently declared that he was both "Muslim and Marxist". In left-wing Algeria, a country committed to a policy of rapid industrialization based on imported western technology, the popular strength of Islam was demonstrated when the metal-workers demanded that the government "broaden the teaching of the true, austere and militant Islam". Islamic societies and youth groups have sprung up everywhere, and political movements such as the fanatical Muslim Brotherhood, originally founded in Egypt in the 1920s, have re-emerged and have gained new adherents. Supporters of the Muslim Brotherhood, regarded by some as the Arab world's most powerful society, were involved in sectarian massacres and killings in Syria during 1979 which shook the ruling Alawite regime. In Egypt tension between the Muslim Brothers and the government mounted after the Camp David agreements, and the Brotherhood is known to have established extensive relations with the *Fedayeen-e-Islam*, one of the oldest guerrilla groups in Iran.

For some observers this Islamic resurgence results from the social disruption brought about by the impact of sudden oil wealth and rapid modernization. Some point to the growing influence of the so-called "reactionary regimes" like Saudi Arabia and the Gulf shaikhdoms and accuse them of using petrodollars to promote Islam as the enemy of change. Others believe that Islam has always been there, strong and alive, and that the present "revival" should be seen more as a rejection of those western ideas and ideologies that have been thrust into an area where they do not belong.

Because of the publicity given to such strict punishments as stoning for adultery, amputation for theft and flogging for drink offences, Islam has earned a reputation in the western world for being harsh and unforgiving. It undoubtedly does have a stern side, which the west finds easy to condemn as barbaric. But the other side of the coin is that the Islamic extended family system provides social welfare, particularly for the old and the needy, in a way which is more efficient and humane than in some developed countries.

The astonishing rise to power of the Ayatollah Khomeini in 1979 on a tidal wave of religious opposition to the pro-western regime of the Shah of Iran had an enormous impact throughout the Middle East. It threw much of the region

71   Hassan El Banna who in the 1920s founded the fanatical Muslim Brotherhood in Egypt. In the 1970s the Muslim Brotherhood re-emerged and gained many new adherents throughout the Arab World.

into an emotional and intellectual turmoil, and many observers predicted that Iran's Islamic revolution would spark off revolutions elsewhere. In the Arab world most of the established order fear Khomeini and all that he stands for. Most of those who want to sweep the existing regimes away welcome him. But beyond that there is much paradox and confusion because within the established order it is the most Islamic regimes who are most afraid, while some of the least Islamic are the most enthusiastic. "After Khomeini", a writer in the Beirut newspaper *Al-Safir* speculated, "no-one can claim to hold the major key to our problems".

But does Khomeini have an answer to the problems which beset the Middle East or is he merely a symptom of nostalgic escapism? Can his attempt to create a theocratic new order, inspired and regulated down to the smallest detail by Islam, prove any more successful than the westernizing and secular order it replaces? It would be presumptuous at this stage to try to answer these questions.

YOUNG HISTORIAN

1 Think of all the different ways in which events in the Middle East affect all our lives.
2 Outline the growth of either (a) American or (b) Soviet influence in the Middle East.
3 Give an explanation of (a) Nasserism, (b) Baathism.
4 How far-reaching have processes of social change been in the Middle East in the twentieth century?
5 Examine the problems and aspirations of *ONE* Middle Eastern minority group.
6 Explain the significance of the "Islamic Revival".

MAIN EVENTS

1901	First oil concession granted for exploration in Iran.
1908	Oil discovered in Iran.
	The Young Turk Revolution and the restoration of the Ottoman Constitution.
1909	Russian forces invade Iran and occupy Tabriz.
1911	Italy attacks Tripoli and proclaims her sovereignty over the Ottoman province of Tripolitania (Libya).
1914	The Ottoman Empire enters First World War on the side of Germany.
	Britain assumes a protectorate over Egypt.
1916	Sharif Husain of Mecca proclaims the Arab revolt against Ottoman rule.
	The Sykes-Picot Agreement to divide the Ottoman Empire into French and British spheres of influence.
1917	Balfour Declaration on the Jewish national home in Palestine.
1918	End of the First World War. The Ottoman Sultan signs an armistice with the victorious Allies.
1919	Victorious Allies convene a Peace Conference in Paris at the end of the First World War.
	Greek army lands at Izmir for the invasion of Anatolia.
	Turkish resistance movement begins under the leadership of Mustafa Kemal (Atatürk).
1920	Treaty of Sèvres partitions the remaining territories of the Ottoman Empire.
	Emir Faisal proclaims the independent kingdom of Greater Syria.
1921	Turkish army under Mustafa Kemal defeats Greeks at Battle of Sakarya.
1922	Ottoman Sultanate abolished. The end of the Ottoman Empire.
	Mustafa Kemal proclaimed first President of the Turkish Republic.
	Treaty of Lausanne re-establishes complete and undivided Turkish sovereignty over the new Turkish Republic.
	Britain proclaims the end of the protectorate over Egypt.
1923	Reza Khan becomes Prime Minister of Iran.
	Britain's Mandate for Palestine confirmed by the League of Nations.
1925	Qajar dynasty deposed and Reza Khan proclaimed Shah of Iran.
1926	Abdul Aziz Ibn Sa'ud conquers the Hejaz, formally marking the establishment of the Saudi Arabian kingdom.
1936	General strike in Palestine called by the Mufti of Jerusalem and the Higher Arab Committee.
1937	British White Paper on Palestine proposes a limit on Jewish immigration.
1938	Death of Mustafa Kemal (Atatürk).
1939	Sanjak of Alexandretta ceded to Turkey.

1941	Reza Shah abdicates.
1942	Extraordinary Zionist Conference held at the Biltmore Hotel, New York.
1946	King David Hotel in Jerusalem blown up by Zionist forces.
	Democrat Party of Turkey founded.
1947	United Nations proposes the partition of Palestine between Arabs and Jews.
1948	British troops withdraw from Palestine.
	Jewish authorities in Palestine proclaim the State of Israel.
	First Arab-Israeli War.
1949	Armistice agreements concluded between Israel and her Arab neighbours.
	Military coup d'état in Syria.
	Baath party founded by Michel Aflaq.
1950	Democrat Party wins Turkish elections.
1951	Iranian oil industry nationalized by the government of Dr Musaddiq.
1952	The Egyptian revolution.
1953	Prime Minister Musaddiq of Iran overthrown by army coup.
1954	Nasser becomes President of Egypt.
1956	The Suez Crisis.
	Palestinian guerrilla organization *Al Fatah* founded.
1958	Egypt and Syria form the United Arab Republic.
	The Iraqi revolution and the overthrow of the monarchy.
1960	The Organization of Petroleum Exporting Countires (OPEC) established.
	The Turkish army overthrows the Democrat government.
1961	Syria leaves the United Arab Republic after army takeover.
1964	Palestine Liberation Organization (PLO) established.
1965	Justice Party under their new leader, Süleyman Demirel, wins the Turkish elections.
1967	The Six Day War.
	United Nations Resolution 242 on Middle East peace.
1969	Military coup in Libya. King deposed by young army officers led by Colonel Muammar Gaddafi.
1970	"Black September". Jordanian army attacks Palestinian commandos and Jordan is thrown into civil war.
	Death of President Nasser of Egypt.
1971	Federation of Arab Republics founded by Egypt, Libya and Syria.
	Turkish army overthrows Demirel's government.
1972	President Sadat of Egypt expels Soviet military advisers.
1973	Return to civilian party politics in Turkey.
	The October or Yom Kippur War.
	Arab oil producers employ the "oil weapon".
1974	First Disengagement Agreement concluded between Egypt and Israel.
	President Makarios of Cyprus overthrown.
	Turkish army invades Cyprus.
	UN General Assembly recognizes the PLO as the representative of the Palestinian people.
	Yasser Arafat, Chairman of the PLO, addresses the UN General Assembly.
1975	Turkish Cypriots declare "Turkish Federated State of Cyprus".
	Second Disengagement Agreement concluded between Egypt and Israel.
	Outbreak of civil war in Lebanon.
1976	Syria invades Lebanon.
1977	Gaddafi proclaims the Libyan Arab Socialist People's Jamahiriya.
	Armed clashes between Egypt and Libya.
	The right-wing Likud party led by Menachem Begin wins the Israeli elections.

President Sadat of Egypt visits Jerusalem and addresses the Israeli Knesset.

Violence erupts in Iran in protest against the Shah's regime.

978 Ecevit, leader of the Republican People's Party, forms new Turkish government.

Israeli invasion of southern Lebanon.

Egypt and Israel sign the Camp David Agreements.

979 Shah leaves Iran.

Ayatollah Khomeini returns to Iran to become *de facto* ruler of Iran's new Islamic republic.

Egypt and Israel sign a peace treaty.

GLOSSARY

Alawites	a small extremist Shi'a sect concentrated in northwest Syria. Key figures in the present (1980) Syrian government, including the president, belong to this sect.
Armenians	a Christian national minority with their own church, language and customs.
Assyrians	a small Christian sect principally found in Iraq and Syria, with their own Aramaic dialect.
Ayatollah	a high-ranking title conferred by the community on senior Muslim theologians, by general acclaim for their learning and service to the community; peculiar to Shi'a Islam.
Caliph, Caliphate	"Caliph" was the title given to the successors of the Prophet Mohamed as the spiritual head of Islam.
Capitulations	a series of treaties granted by the Ottoman Sultans to various European countries, giving their nationals immunity to Ottoman law.
Circassians	a Christian national minority.
Copts	native Christians of Egypt, Arabic speaking, but using the Coptic language in church services.
détente	easing of strained relations, especially between states.
dervish	a member of an Islamic religious brotherhood.
Druzes	a small religious sect in Syria, Lebanon and Palestine. It is an offshoot of Shi'a Islam, though its beliefs and practices differ widely from Muslim orthodoxy.
EOKA	in Greek, "National Organization of the Struggle for the Freedom of Cyprus". A Greek Cypriot guerrilla group, founded in 1954, and extreme advocates of Enosis or union with Greece.
étatism	state capitalism.
fedayeen	in Arabic literally "those who sacrifice their lives", recently used to describe bands of guerrilla fighters.
Fertile Crescent	the area of fertile land stretching from the coast of Israel through northwest Syria to the Tigris-Euphrates valley.
Grand Vezir	Chief Minister of the Ottoman Empire.
Gush Emunim	"Bloc of the Faithful", an extreme religious Zionist group.
Hashemites	the family which held the hereditary title of Sharif of Mecca from the twelfth century until 1924. Two sons of the last Sharif (Husain) became kings of Jordan (Abdullah) and Iraq (Faisal).
Hejaz	the western coastal strip of modern Saudi Arabia which includes the holy cities of Mecca and Medina.

92

Imam	a descendant of the Prophet, spiritual leader of the Shi'a Muslims and in Yemen head of state until 1962.
Islam	literally "resignation to the will of God". A religion based on the Koran, the holy book revealed to Mohamed, the Prophet in the seventh century AD.
Janissaries	an élite military corps in the Ottoman army recruited from among the Sultan's Christian subjects.
Kataeb (Phalangists)	literally "battalion"; an extreme right-wing Christian political group in Lebanon with its own paramilitary organization.
Khedive	originally a Persian word meaning "lord". It was adopted by the governor of Egypt, Ismail, in 1841 when the office of Pasha of Egypt was made hereditary in his family as a more prestigious title.
Kurds	a Sunni Muslim national minority with their own language and customs.
Majlis	literally "council"; a consultative assembly of notables or elected representatives.
Maronites	an Arab Christian sect affiliated to the Roman Catholic Church, Arabic-speaking but using Aramaic in public worship; chiefly in the Lebanon.
Mesopotamia	the lower valleys of the Tigris and Euphrates.
millet	the status of *millet* was granted to the major non-Muslim religious communities of the Ottoman Empire by which they enjoyed a considerable measure of internal autonomy.
Mufti	an official Muslim expert in Islamic law who was also a dignitary of some standing in the major cities of the Ottoman Empire.
mullah	a local Muslim authority on Islamic law and religion.
Pasha	the highest honorific official title in the Ottoman Empire.
Qajars	the ruling dynasty of Persia from 1756—1925
Ramadan	ninth month of the Muslim year which is observed by Muslims as a strict fast from dawn to sunset each day of the month.
Safavids	the ruling dynasty of Persia (Iran) during the sixteenth and seventeenth centuries.
Sanjak	an administrative district and subdivision of an Ottoman province.
shaikh	honorary title of head of a tribe or clan. Courtesy title of theological scholars, notables and local dignitaries.
Sharia	holy law of Islam as revealed in the Koran and traditions of Mohamed.
Sharif	a title used to signify a descendant of the Prophet Mohamed. Title given to the guardian of the Holy Cities, Mecca and Medina, under the Ottoman Empire.
Shi'a Muslims	literally the "party of Ali" (the Prophet's son-in-law), now the principal heterodox religious group within Islam, as distinct from Sunni (orthodox) Muslims. Found mainly in Iran and southern Iraq.
Sunni Muslims	the majority group of, or orthodox Muslims.
wafd	in Arabic "delegation". The name adopted by one of the early Egyptian nationalist parties.
Wahhabi Movement	a movement of religious reform in Islam founded in the eighteenth century, aiming at a return to purity and simplicity of early Islam. A major influence in the modern Kingdom of Saudi Arabia.
Yom Kippur	"Day of Atonement" — a Jewish one-day fast, the most holy day in their religious calendar.

BOOKS FOR FURTHER READING

Abbott, A.J., *The Iranians, How they Live and Work* (David & Charles, 1977)

Adams, M. (ed.), *The Middle East: a handbook* (Blond, 1971)

Altounyan, Taqui, *In Aleppo Once* (Murray, 1969)

Bar-Zohar, Michael, *Ben Gurion*, trans. P. Kidron (Weidenfeld & Nicolson, 1978)

Beckingham, C.F., *Atlas of the Arab World and the Middle East* (Macmillan, 1960)

Bedoukian, Kerop, *The Urchin: an Armenian's escape* (Murray, 1978)

Bianco, Mirella, *Gadafi: voice from the desert*, tr. M. Lyle (Longman, 1975)

Bulloch, John, *Death of a Country, The Civil War in Lebanon* (Weidenfeld & Nicolson, 1977)

Dimbleby, J. & McCullin, D., *The Palestinians* (Quartet Books, 1979)

Field, M., *A hundred million dollars a day* (Sidgwick & Jackson, 1975)

Glubb, Sir John, *The Course of Empire: the Arabs and their Successors* (Hodder & Stoughton, 1965)

Guillaume, Alfred, *Islam* (2nd rev. edition) (Penguin Books, 1956)

Harper, S., *The Last Sunset* (Collins, 1978)

Heikal, Mohamed, *Nasser. The Cairo Documents* (New English Library Ltd, 1972)

Hirst, David, *The Gun & the Olive Branch: the roots of violence in the Middle East* (Faber, 1977)

Holden, D., *Farewell to Arabia* (Faber & Faber, 1966)

Kirk, G.E., *A Short History of the Middle East* (Methuen, 1948)

Mango, Andrew, *Turkey* (Thames & Hudson, 1968)

Nutting, Sir Anthony, *No end of a lesson, the Story of Suez* (Constable, 1967)

Woollacott, Martin, *The Changing Dream* (Guardian Newspapers Ltd, 1979)

INDEX

The numbers in **bold type** are the figure numbers of the illustrations

אוסף